Culture as Curriculum

Alan R. Sadovnik and Susan F. Semel
General Editors

Vol. 2

The History of Schools and Schooling series
is part of the Peter Lang Education list.
Every volume is peer reviewed and meets
the highest quality standards for content and production.

PETER LANG
New York • Washington, D.C./Baltimore • Bern
Frankfurt • Berlin • Brussels • Vienna • Oxford

Eugene F. Provenzo, Jr.

Culture as Curriculum

Education and the International Expositions (1876–1904)

PETER LANG
New York • Washington, D.C./Baltimore • Bern
Frankfurt • Berlin • Brussels • Vienna • Oxford

Library of Congress Cataloging-in-Publication Data
Provenzo, Eugene F.
Culture as curriculum: education and the international expositions (1876–1904) /
Eugene F. Provenzo, Jr.
p. cm. — (History of schools and schooling; v. 2)
Includes bibliographical references and index.
1. Education—United States—History—19th century. 2. Education—United States—
History—20th century. 3. Centennial Exhibition (1876: Philadelphia, Pa.)
4. World's Columbian Exposition (1893: Chicago, Ill.)
5. Louisiana Purchase Exposition (1904: Saint Louis, Mo.) I. Title.
LA216.P76   370.973—dc23   2012030243
ISBN 978-0-8204-3398-1 (paperback)
ISBN 978-1-4539-0891-4 (e-book)
ISBN 978-0-8204-3398-1
ISSN 1089-0678

Bibliographic information published by **Die Deutsche Nationalbibliothek**.
Die Deutsche Nationalbibliothek lists this publication in the "Deutsche
Nationalbibliografie"; detailed bibliographic data is available
on the Internet at http://dnb.d-nb.de/.

Cover image: "Ready to Admit the World," Howard J. Rogers,
Chief of the Department of Education at the Louisiana Purchase Exposition,
cover of the *School Board Journal*, 24, no. 5, May 1904.

© 2012 Peter Lang Publishing, Inc., New York
29 Broadway, 18th floor, New York, NY 10006
www.peterlang.com

All rights reserved.
Reprint or reproduction, even partially, in all forms such as microfilm,
xerography, microfiche, microcard, and offset strictly prohibited.

Contents

Acknowledgments vii

Chapter One. Introduction.. 1

Chapter Two. The Philadelphia Centennial Exhibition:. 13

Chapter Three. The World's Columbian Exposition 63

Chapter Four. The Louisiana Purchase Exposition........................... 97

Conclusion. Culture as Curriculum 129

Bibliography..137

Index 153

Acknowledgments

This is a book about education and its role in the construction of culture. As such, it fits within the traditions of not only educational history, but also cultural studies. I began the book many years ago as part of a broader interest on my part in the role of the International Expositions in American and world culture. I have been helped by numerous people in this research, most importantly my wife, Asterie Baker Provenzo, who accompanied me to archives and libraries across the country in search of materials, as well as being my companion in life, editor and best friend.

Special thanks go to Alan Sadovnik and Susan Semel for their support and interest in this project and my work as an educational historian.

Over the years, as I collected information about various international expositions, my parents Gene and Terri Provenzo would search out exposition catalogues and memorabilia for me in bookstores and antique stores. Their enthusiasm in finding resources for my research was a source of great pleasure for me. It is in their memory that I dedicate this book.

Eugene F. Provenzo, Jr.
University of Miami
Summer 2011

Chapter 1
Introduction

The Dynamo at the Paris 1900 Exposition. Courtesy of the Library of Congress.

The decades following the Civil War saw the United States transformed from an agrarian into an urban and industrialized society. Innovation and rapid change characterized the period. New methods of production, mechanized farming and the growth of more effective means of transportation and communication were redefining the lives of the American people.

The confusion of these decades has been touched upon by many scholars, but perhaps none with as much insight as the American historian Henry Adams. Adams realized that industry and invention were merging together as a single powerful force—one that was creating a new social and moral order. Standing in the Gallery of Machines at the 1900 Paris Exposition, Adams realized that he was witnessing in the exhibits of the various engines and dynamos the spirit of a new age. Speaking in third person, he later wrote:

> ...to Adams, the dynamo became a symbol of infinity. As he grew accustomed to the great gallery of machines, he began to feel the forty-foot dynamos as a moral force, much as the early Christian felt the Cross. The planet itself seemed less impressive, in its old fashioned, deliberate annual or daily revolution, than this huge wheel revolving at arm's-length at some vertiginous speed, and barely murmuring—scarcely humming an audible warning to stand a hair's breath for respect of power—while it would not wake the baby lying close against its frame. Before the end, one began to pray to it; inherited instinct taught the natural expression of man silent and infinite force. Among the thousand symbols of ultimate energy, the dynamo was not so human as some but it was the most expressive.[1]

The great international expositions of the late nineteenth and early twentieth centuries were reflections of this new force. The expositions brought together the world's political, intellectual and industrial leaders for the exchange of information and ideas. At the same time they had imbedded within their organization and exhibits specific social and cultural agendas and schools for promoting specific cultural and ideological points of view. These expositions, from the Great London Exhibition of 1851 and through the 1904 St. Louis Louisiana Purchase Exposition, reflected the preoccupations and interests of the individuals who organized and contributed to their exhibits. Although geographically diverse and separated from one another by the passage of time, the expositions were unified by at least one consistent theme—the relationship of knowledge and power. As J. George Hodgins, the Ontario Commissioner of Education for the 1876 Philadelphia Centennial Exhibition explained, the:

> ...great international Exhibitions were the first grand levers which were used to uplift the nations to a higher plane of intellectual life, and to demonstrate

to them, beyond power of controversy to gainsay, the great practical truth which underlies the trite maxim which we all understand, that "knowledge is indeed power"—power which is irresistible—power, which with unerring penetration and force, seizes upon salient points; and, by controlling, turns even opposing forces into obedient servants of a superior will and design.²

London Exhibition, 1851—End View. From: *Frank Leslie's Historical Register of the Centennial Exposition*, p. 3.

In the United States, this equation of knowledge and power was a response to the new industrial order—one which saw with it the emergence of a new political and economic leadership whose influence was rooted in their control of finances and technology. When the Philadelphia Centennial Exhibition opened in 1876, the American continent had been spanned by the railroads and the telegraph. The Frontier had been subdued, if not conquered, by the farmers with their mechanical reapers and by the ranchers and their barbed wire. The power of the Frontier as a force within American culture was diminishing. New industries and means of production were redefining the traditional economy. Knowledge essential to industrial and technological development represented a new frontier to be explored—one which brought with it a new type of power.

The international expositions both in the United States and abroad were instruments and reflections of this new power. As such, they represented manifestations of the nineteenth century's faith in scientific and material progress. Ultimately, they were schools to which the nations of the world came to learn the equation of knowledge and power. As Henry Adams observed at the 1904 Louisiana Purchase Exposition:

> The chaos of education approached a dream. One asked one's self whether this extravagance reflected the past or imagined the future; whether it was a creation of the old American or a promise of the new one. No prophet could be believed, but a pilgrim of power, without constituency to flatter, might allow himself to hope. The prospect of the Exposition was pleasant; one seemed to see almost an adequate motive for power; almost a scheme for progress.[3]

Perhaps nowhere was the impact of the expositions and the new systems of knowledge and power they helped to set in place as great as in the area of education. Each of the major international expositions held in the United States, beginning in 1876 with the Philadelphia Centennial Exhibition and continuing with the Worlds Columbian Exposition in Chicago in 1893 and the 1904 St. Louis Louisiana Purchase Exposition, included major educational exhibits and congresses.

It is the thesis of this work that the international expositions and the educational exhibits and congresses that were held under their auspices were to have an important role in shaping reforms and innovations in American education during the late nineteenth and early twentieth centuries, and that many of the values that these exhibits, together with the overall schemes of the expositions of which they were a part, represented a symbolic universe constructed by an emerging economic and social elite—an elite who reflected not only specific economic and class interests, but a belief in the inherent superiority of White Anglo-Saxon American culture.

In doing so, the expositions represented an "exercise of economic and political power in cultural terms by the established leaders of American society," one which was spontaneously consented to by the great majority of the American people.[4] In this context, the expositions were instruments of social, political and cultural hegemony.[5]

The notion of the expositions serving a hegemonic function has been examined by Robert Rydell in his ground-breaking study *All the World's a Fair: Visions of Empire at American International Expositions, 1876–1916*. According to Rydell, through their architecture, organization and the selection of subjects to be exhibited, the:

> World's fairs performed a hegemonic function precisely because they propagated the ideas and values of the country's political, financial, corporate, and

intellectual leaders and offered these ideas as the proper interpretation of social and political reality.[6]

In this work I will demonstrate how hegemonic forces—ones that represented very specific views concerning race and the relationship between knowledge and power—were reflected not only in the content of the educational exhibits, but in the more general rhetoric and organization of the expositions. While educational theorists such as Michael Apple and others have discussed in great detail how schools function to make and remake a dominant culture—and of the hegemonic functions they serve—virtually all of their work has focused on contemporary education.[7] Little attention has been given to historical studies of hegemony and education. This work represents an attempt to provide such a study.[8]

It is assumed that the great international expositions of the nineteenth century, like the schools, functioned as instruments of social, political and cultural hegemony and that hegemony acts to "saturate" our consciousness. That it is:

> ...a whole body of practices and expectations; our assignments of energy, our ordinary understanding of man and his world. It is a set of meaning and values which as they are experienced as practices appear as reciprocally confirming. It thus constitutes a sense of reality for most people in the society, a sense of absolute because experienced [as a] reality beyond which it is very difficult for most members of a society to move in most areas of their lives. But this is not, except in the operation of a moment of abstract analysis, a static system. On the contrary we can only understand an effective and dominant culture if we understand the real social process on which it depends: I mean the process of incorporation.[9]

This work is a study in the field of educational history, but like Bernard Bailyn and Lawrence Cremin it assumes that education goes beyond just what occurs in the schools and also includes institutions such as the family, libraries, museums and the media.[10] In this context, although the primary focus of this study will be on the educational exhibits relating to public and private schooling, attention will also be given to broader subjects such as the development of museums and libraries that were also influenced by the educational exhibits and congresses held in conjunction with the expositions.

In many respects this is a work in "historical archaeology." Through the use of photographs, catalogue illustrations and text sources I will attempt to reconstruct what the actual educational exhibits at the expositions were like, as well as to comment on their significance for American culture and education. This work is limited in that it deals with the educational exhibits of three of the international expositions that were held in the United States. Arguments could be made that other American and European expositions should have been included as well. The exclusion of the 1901 Pan American Exposition in Buffalo may, for example, be considered a serious oversight. In collecting the data for this study, however, the author became convinced that the significant fairs, in terms of education, were the ones held in Philadelphia in 1876, in Chicago in 1893 and in St. Louis in 1904.[11]

The international expositions were a special creation of the second half of the nineteenth century. Major international expositions of the type held in Philadelphia, Chicago and St. Louis no longer exist. Too often these expositions are confused with the modern world's fairs. The twentieth century's world's fairs are much more of a trade fair than the nineteenth century expositions. The conventions and learned congresses that were such an important part of the expositions are not a part of the modern world's fairs.

Although different types of commercial and industrial exhibits were held in England and France during the late eighteenth and early nineteenth centuries, none of these were international in scope. It was not until 1851 that Prince Albert, the consort of Queen Victoria, convinced the members of the Society of Arts, along with a group of English businessmen and political leaders, that a commercial and industrial exposition being held in Hyde Park should be opened to foreign visitors. It was Prince Albert's belief that such an exposition would not only contribute to the cause of international peace by bringing together various European nations in a cooperative effort, but that the comparison of English manufactured goods with those of countries such as France would encourage the English to adopt more sophisticated industrial methods and designs for their own work.[12]

The Great London Exhibition of 1851, or as it is more commonly known, the "Crystal Palace Exhibition," did not include any educational exhibits. Yet despite this fact, the exhibition was to have a major impact on English education. In 1851, as a direct outgrowth of the exhibition, the South Kensington Museum was established in order to provide a showplace and museum for outstanding examples of international manufacture and design. In conjunction with the museum the School for Industrial Art was established—the first school of its type to be set up in England.[13] Additions were made to the museum after each major international exposition. In 1854, for example, educational materials at St. Martin's Hall were brought to the South Kensington Museum in order to form the nucleus for a permanent pedagogical exhibit.[14]

London Exhibition, 1851—Transept. From: *Frank Leslie's Historical Register of the Centennial Exposition*, p. 3.

Although important international expositions were held in Paris in 1855 and London in 1852, it was not until the Paris Exposition of 1867 that education received attention as a special subject of interest.[15] Assigned to the "Department of Social Science," the educational exhibit included materials from nearly twelve-hundred different sources. Of these, half were from France and the remainder from countries such as England, Belgium, Prussia, Sweden and Denmark.[16] The exhibit was enormous. According to J. W. Hoyt, the American Educational Commissioner to the Exposition, it extended:

> ...through the whole range appropriate to the work of education, and affording ground for a discussion of every educational theme, from the material appliances essential to the infant school, up through every grade of intermediate schools, general and special, to the scheme of the Royal Academy of the University.[17]

As observed by Hoyt, the educational exhibits at the Paris Exposition elicited widespread interest among French educators. By the end of the exposition over 12,000 French school teachers had gone to Paris in order to view the educational exhibit.

The success of the Parisian exhibit encouraged the commissioners of the 1873 Viennese Exposition to make education an important part of their exhibits. A total of over five-thousand exhibitors submitted materials for display as part of the educational exhibit at Vienna. Twenty different nations were represented. Among the exhibits which received the greatest attention was a complete rural school building from the United States. Furnished with a teacher's table, desks for the students, a harmonium, reference books and textbooks, the building and its contents provided a working model that could be compared with European schools buildings and educational materials. In addition, photographs of various public institutions were included as part of the American exhibit, including asylums for the Deaf and Dumb, the Blind and the Insane, as well as the architectural designs of public school buildings from towns such as St. Louis and Washington, D.C.[18]

Machinery Hall at the 1873 Vienna Exposition.

The educational exhibit included at Vienna was well received. Commenting on the exhibit and the work of its director Baron Schwarz Senborn, John Eaton, the American Commissioner of Education explained that:

> The programs of the Department of Education at Vienna produced upon my mind a most forcible impression. The breadth of view, the all comprehensive

grasp of the subject, worked out with such perfection of detail, gave evidence that a mind of no ordinary calibre had originated this noble conception... It seemed the scheme of a great philanthropic statesmen [sic], planning for the advancement of his own people, but broad enough to include all of the people of the world, who were freely invited to come to Vienna and see the results of civilization.[19]

It is in this context that the international expositions and their educational exhibits are of greatest interest. The expositions provided educators with a forum where they could freely exchange ideas and observe the educational experiments of other nations. In doing so, they were achieving the primary purpose intended by the organizers of the expositions—the exchange and advancement of new technical information and knowledge. At the same time, they represented a clearly articulated vision of culture—one reflecting a specific cultural, political and social hegemony. As such, the expositions were neither neutral, nor simply the scheme of philanthropic statesmen and educators, but were powerful instruments of knowledge and power reflecting increasingly dominant hegemonic forces within American and world culture.

Notes

1. Henry Adams, *The Education of Henry Adams* (New York: The Modern Library, 1931), p. 380.
2. J. George Hodgins, *Special Report to the Honorable The Minister of Education, On the Ontario Educational Exhibit, And the Educational Features of the International Exhibition, At Philadelphia, 1876* (Toronto, ON: Hunter, Rose & Co., 1877), pp. 231-232.
3. Adams, op. cit., p. 467.
4. Robert Rydell, *All the World's a Fair: Visions of Empire at American International Expositions, 1876-1916* (Chicago: University of Chicago Press, 1984), p. 2.
5. Ibid.

    Significantly, Rydell points out that: Hegemony, moreover, is the normal means of state control in a pluralistic society; force is used when power exercised in cultural terms is no long capable of maintain the order on which the state is founded. (*Ibid.*)
6. Ibid., p. 3.
7. My understanding of hegemony and its implications for education is based largely upon the work of Michael Apple. See his studies: *Ideology and Curriculum* (London: Routledge & Kegan Paul, 1979); *Cultural and Economic Reproduction in Education: Essays on Class, Ideology and the State*, editor (London: Routledge & Kegan Paul, 1982); Michael W. Apple, *Education and Power* (Boston: Routledge & Kegan Paul,

Introduction   11

8. 1983); and Michael W. Apple and Lois Weis, editors, *Ideology and Practice in Schooling* (Philadelphia: Temple University Press, 1983).
8. Hegemony is a difficult concept to clearly define. Raymond Williams in his essay "Base and Superstructure in Marxist Cultural Theory," included in *Schooling and Capitalism: A Sociological Reader* (London: Routledge & Kegan Paul, 1976), pp. 204-205, provides some help when describing the work of the Italian Marxist Antonio Gramsci:

> ...hegemony supposes the existence of something which is truly total, which is not merely secondary or superstructural, like the weak sense of ideology, but which is lived at such depth, which saturates the society to such an extent, and which, as Gramsci put it, even constitutes the limit of commonsense for most people under its sway.

9. *Ibid.*, p. 205.
10. See: Bernard Bailyn, *Education and the Forming of American Society* (New York: Norton, 1972). This is also the assumption of Lawrence Cremin's three-volume study *American Education*. See Cremin: *American Education: The Colonial Experience, 1607-1783* (New York: Harper and Row, 1970); *American Education: The National Experience, 1783-1876* (New York: Harper and Row, 1980); and *American Education: The Metropolitan Experience, 1876-1980* (New York: Harper and Row, 1988).
11. While education was included in other exhibits, both here and abroad, I have deliberately decided to limit myself to these three American settings. In a sense this work may be considered a series of historical case studies—although I am convinced they are the most important cases available.
12. See: J. S. Ingram, *The Centennial Exposition* (Philadelphia: Hubbard Bros., 1876), pp. 28-29. Also see: *The Great Exhibition, London* (Facsimile of the 1851 *Art Journal Illustrated Catalogue of the Industries of All Nations* (New York: Crown Books, 1970).
13. Percy Atkin, "Popular Education in England," in *National Educational Association of the United States, Addresses and Proceedings* (St. Louis, 1904) (Wiona, MN: National Educational Association, 1904), pp. 83-88. Both English and foreign writers throughout the latter part of the nineteenth century ascribed the revival of English arts and manufactures to the interest in design stimulated by the 1851 Exhibition. See for example, the discussion by I. Edwards Clarke in *Art and Industry: Industrial and High Art Education in the United States* (Washington, DC: Government Printing Office, 1885), pp. xciv-xcv.
14. Richard Waterman, Jr., "Educational Exhibits at World's Fairs Since 1851 (I)," *Educational Review*, 5, February 1893, p. 123.
15. Hodgins, *op. cit.*, p. 1.
16. *Ibid.*
17. *Ibid.*, p. 2 (Hodgins quoting Hoyt).

18. Richard Waterman, Jr., "Educational Exhibits at World's Fairs Since 1851 (II)," *Educational Review*, 5, March 1893, pp. 222–223.
19. Quoted by Hodgins, *op. cit.*, p. 3.

Chapter 2
The Philadelphia Centennial Exhibition

President Grant and Dom Pedro starting the Corliss Engine, *Harper's Weekly*, May 27, 1876, p. 421.

The Philadelphia Centennial Exhibition symbolized America's coming of age. Celebrating the hundredth anniversary of the founding of the Republic, it not only reflected on the accomplishments of the past, but anticipated the possibilities of the future. The United States and its technological methods and discoveries that were laying the foundation of a new industrial era were exhibited before the world.

Early on, it was recognized that education should play an important role in the Centennial Exhibition. At the beginning of 1874, the Superintendent's Department of the National Education Association recommended that the various states and territories, as well as cities, prepare historical exhibits about their schools and displays of their current work. In addition, it was suggested that invitations be sent to prominent educators throughout the world asking that they participate in the Centennial Exhibition, and that an International Congress of Education be held in conjunction with the exhibits.[1]

Throughout 1875 John Eaton issued a series of circulars outlining the types of materials wanted for the educational exhibits, as well as the procedures to be followed in preparing them for display.[2] Further detailed instructions were provided to potential exhibitors by the United States Bureau of Education. The hundreds of letters written in 1875 and 1876 by Eaton to potential exhibitors about assembling and shipping exhibits attest to the attention given to the educational exhibits.[3]

The response to Eaton's call for educational materials was positive. Numerous foreign countries and colonial possessions responded by sending materials for display. State and local school boards, in conjunction with their school systems, began to assemble materials for the exhibits. Local and regional pride often influenced the selection of materials. Underlying the desire of many American exhibitors to put together comprehensive and informative exhibits was the need to demonstrate the superiority of American schools. In a circular distributed in Connecticut asking for educational materials for the Connecticut school exhibit, for example, it was explained that:

> ...European visitors will attach special importance to our educational exhibit. They will ask what has the nation accomplished educationally during the first hundred years of its growth, and what visible results can it show. To disappoint them would be humiliating. To merit and receive their commendation will give a new impulse to the cause of education throughout the land.[4]

President Grant opening the Exhibition, *Harper's Weekly*, May 27, 1876, p. 425.

The honor of the American people was clearly at stake. As Eaton explained:

> ...the Centennial should be altogether a school of patriotism, illustrating the excellence of the American system of government by the people, for the people, and that education, as the primary cause of these excellencies should be fully represented....[5]

For the American people, education was clearly associated with the idea of patriotism, a fact observed by at least one visitor to the Centennial Exposition. M. Ferdinand Buisson, the commissioner in charge of the French educational exhibit at the Centennial argued that many Americans saw their country's political future as being dependent upon the effectiveness of its schools. As Buisson observed, the Americans

> ...flatter themselves that by a better training of the rising generation, and by giving the children of the lower social classes an education worthy of free citizens, they will gradually diminish both the number of intriguers and the number of dupes. This preoccupation, which in absence of anything better, is a sort of American patriotism, contributes more than we are able to tell to keep up the interest in the schools.[6]

Likewise, Buisson observed that economic development was linked to education:

> If the political future of the United States depends on the efficiency of her schools, her commercial future is no less directly interested. The conditions of labor in the New World are such that success depends, as it were, on a certain degree of education. In industrial, commercial, agricultural, financial, or other occupations, the success of each will be almost in proportion to his intelligence.[7]

Buisson was describing the tradition of the "self-made man," and with it the emergence of a new commercial and industrial culture.[8] Personal initiative was the key to this new civilization and ultimately to progress and power in America. In turn, education was the key to initiative:

> The spirit of initiative, of enterprise, of adventure, even, is the result of this entirely new civilization; there is no American without the "go ahead." ...Under these circumstances education has a double value: it has besides its real value a kind of surplus value, resulting from its practical and commercial usefulness. The whole political economy of the United States takes this for granted; without it, neither the farmer nor the business man would be able to calculate his chances of success; the artisan and the laborer would not endeavor to improve their work, to lessen their hardships, or to increase their profits. The wealth of the United States is incalculable precisely because intellectual wealth counts for an enormous proportion.[9]

Visitors to the Centennial constantly compared the technological achievements of the United States and Europe with those of Asia. Europe and America were seen as representing the dynamic forces of progress and invention at work, while Asia represented traditionalism and imitation. Invention was clearly viewed as a moral virtue, while imitation was seen as a sign of decadence. B. G. Northrup, the Secretary to the Connecticut Board of Education observed that: "Invention implies increase of power and growth of ideas and character. Mere imitation keeps a nation repeating itself for ages."[10]

Invention for Northrup was immediately dependent upon education. As he explained:

> This tendency on our part to the invention of machines and appliances which confer on our society new power, and to the bringing forward of new ideas which uplift whole communities into a higher stage of existence, and into broader fields of influence may be largely attributed to the nature and breadth of our popular education.[11]

"The Nation's Birthday," *Harper's Weekly*, July, 15, 1876, p. 577. Popular sources such as the cartoonist Thomas Nast represented the United States as represented by Lady Liberty bringing the lessons of democracy to the world.

Education was clearly seen as the means by which to bring about the creation of a new technological and industrial culture in the United States. According to the rhetoric of the era, the rapid growth of the American economy was understood to be dependent upon the inventiveness of its people. This inventiveness was in turn perceived as being a function of their education. It is not surprising therefore that the theme of industry dominated the educational exhibits at the Centennial. The exposition itself was an "educational experience," as well as a manifestation of the new industrial order. As William Torrey Harris, the St. Louis superintendent of schools explained:

> the industry of the world was collected there in its bewildering variety, and not scattered around, but *crowded* into buildings covering fifty acres with some hundreds of miles of avenues lined on both sides with the commodities of human art.[12]

Contemporary accounts of the Centennial Exhibition indicate however, that the educational exhibits were not as successful as had originally been hoped. The Judge's Report laid the blame on the commissioners of the Exposition.[13] Although a Department of Education and Science had been included as one of the three principal departments in the Main Building, it was found upon careful examination that most of the exhibits in the building emphasized science. In an article published in *the New England Journal of Education* H. F. Harrington complained that:

> Scattered, fragmentary, unsystematic, the exhibit of the department of Education produces no unity of impression, and has no powerful suggestive force. It is neither a glory nor an impulse, The displays by Pennsylvania and Massachussetts have decided character, and redound, in various particulars, to the honor of their States; and the lesser displays of some other States have points that are very creditable. But the best State exhibits plainly betray how much they suffer for want of more room and more outlay of money to do them justice.[14]

The reality seems to have been that the general educational exhibits were not of particular interest to the majority of visitors to the Centennial Exhibition.[15] As one anonymous journalist noted:

> Educational exhibits are of minor interest to the great throng. Admiring crowds at all hours stand before Turkish carpets or Gorham silver ware, or surge through the narrow apartments of Memorial Hall, but few are they who care to climb the stairs leading to the galleries in which the most interesting displays are half-hidden from sight.[16]

As might be expected, the education exhibits that attracted the most attention from the public were those which involved the actual display of school buildings and demonstration classes. Among the most popular of these exhibits was the display of a full-size country schoolhouse from Sweden. All of the materials were brought from Sweden and assembled by Swedish carpenters. Designed to accommodate fifty children, the schoolhouse measured forty by fifty feet. In addition to the classroom area, a small apartment was included in the building in which the school master and his family lived. Fully furnished with desks and blackboards, the Swedish school-house included an exhibit of textbooks, as well as detailed catalogues providing information on the different types of schools in Sweden, teachers' salaries and other information related to education.[17]

Visitors in the British section of Memorial Hall, *Harper's Weekly*, December 16, 1876, p. 1012.

Descriptions of the Swedish exhibit by journalists and educators indicate that there was a great deal of interest in it by the general public.[18] Yet the primary importance of the Swedish schoolhouse exhibit lay not in the response to the exhibit by the public, but instead in the example it set for educators in terms of its simplicity and efficient design. The importance of these types of models on display at the expositions cannot be overemphasized. At the exposition in Vienna in 1873, a similar type of building had been exhibited by the Swedes. Commenting on that building John Philbrick, the Superintendent of the Boston Public Schools, recalled how:

> ...I entered the beautiful Swedish School-house, and I took my seat on the Master's platform and surveyed the spectacle presented by the school-room, with its apparatus and fittings, I felt glad that my attempts to bring over a school-room had failed, because I could not have matched what I saw befoe me. I reckon that the State of Massachusetts will get paid for the cost of sending me to Vienna, a hundred times over, by the benefit derived from the knowledge of the idea of school-room (German and Swedish) which I brought home with me.[19]

The Swedish School House. After the Centennial Exhibition Frederick Law Olmstead the designer of New York's Central Park purchased the building and rebuilt it in the park, just east of the Museum of Natural History. The building has served as a puppet theater since the late 1940s. Courtesy of the Free Library of Philadelphia.

It was in this way, through their impact on educational leaders such as Philbrick, that the educational exhibits and congresses held at the expositions were to play a particularly important role in the development of American education during the late nineteenth and early twentieth centuries. Perhaps nowhere is this clearer than in the case of industrial education.

The years immediately preceding the Centennial Exposition were an important period of innovation and experimentation in American and European industrial education. With rapid urbanization and industrialization, increasing demands were placed upon the schools to make the educational experience they provided relevant to the needs of commerce and industry. Educators such as William Torrey Harris saw the United States entering into a new industrial epoch. Perceiving mankind's history as a succession of industrial developmental stages Harris identified the first epoch as being characterized by the use of slave labor. The second epoch had as its purpose

> ...the training of the laborer to a single simple function or activity so as to secure thereby the greatest possible skill and rapidity of production.[20]

According to Harris, this second phase of industrial development was not accompanied by a corresponding enlightenment of the laborer. In concentrating his work on a single function, the laborer was reduced to being little more than a machine. Finally, as Harris explained:

> ...out of the second phase of industry, by a sort of dialectic necessity, proceeds the third. The ultimate tendency of the division of labor is to subdivide each process for the sake of acquiring skill, until a maximum of simplicity is reached.[21]

It was in this third phase that the role of machinery came into play. The simpler the movement, the easier it was to find a substitute for the work of the laborer:

> When a number of simple mechanical processes are discovered, the directing mind of labor begins to invent combinations of machinery and with this enters the third epoch of industry. Machinery continually grows more complex in this epoch, and tends to invade the province of the mere hand-laborer, and to render him useless by providing cheaper and more certain means of accomplishing his work.[22]

The introduction of machinery demanded alertness and versatility on the part of the laborer. As a form of industry it required

> ...general intelligence in the workman as an indespensible basis, and the school education which is thus rendered necessary reacts again upon the industry, making new and subtler combinations of machinery, and continually emancipating the laborer from drudgery.[23]

The United States, as well as many of the European nations, had clearly entered this third industrial phase. Yet despite this fact, no clear philosophy and curriculum for industrial education had emerged. It is not surprising, therefore, that considerable attention was given to the problem of industrial education at the Centennial Exhibition.

Numerous American technical schools exhibited their methods of training as part of the educational exhibits of the various states. The Massachusetts display, for example, included an extensive exhibit of methods and materials used at the Massachusetts Institute of Technology.[24] Similar displays were put together by Stevens Institute of Technology, the Illinois Industrial University and the Worcester County Free Institute of Industrial Science.[25]

Machinery Hall at the Centennial Exhibition—south avenue from west end. Courtesy of the Free Library of Philadelphia.

Except for purposes of comparison, the displays of the American technical schools received relatively little attention from the American educators visiting the exhibition. Instead, it was the exhibit of didactic materials and tools from the technical schools in Moscow and St. Petersburg that captured the interest of the American educators and which was to be responsible for reshaping the character of American industrial education.[26]

The key to the Russian exhibits was found in the examples of drawing and the models and tools illustrating the work of Victor Della Vos at the Moscow Imperial Technical School. Founded in 1830, the school had been reorganized in 1868 under imperial sponsorship. The course on instruction was at the secondary and collegiate levels and took six years to complete. The school's purpose was to train civil and mechanical engineers, draftsmen, industrial foremen and chemists. In addition to the basic theoretical training received by the the students, the school provided them with instruction in wood turning, carpentry, metal turning, fitting and forging.[27]

Della Vos and his staff at the Imperial Technical School wished to provide their students with more than just vocational training in a particular craft. Instead, the purpose of the program was to introduce students to the basic principles of design inherent in crafts such as forging and woodworking. Instruction in manual arts provided a means by which students could visualize and understand abstract design principles. Unlike the older apprenticeship system, emphasis was placed not on the production of objects by the student, but upon understanding the principles of design.

This emphasis on the synthesis of abstract design principles by the student and the application of them to completing a specific task, had important implications for the modern industrial system that had emerged in both Europe and America during the second half of the nineteenth century. Industry demanded adaptability. Problems were not solved by simply following traditional methods. New industrial techniques and materials demanded the careful analysis of information and the adoption of carefully reasoned solutions to specific problems. Della Vos's method clearly addressed the critical problem of how to train specialized technical workers such as draftsmen, chemists, civil and mechancial engineers and industrial foremen to deal with the demands imposed by an increasingly sophisticated and complex industrial system. His purpose was:

> ...to work out such a method of teaching the elementary principles of mechanical art as, firstly, should demand the least possible length of time for their acquirement; secondly, should increase the facility of the supervision of the gradationary employment of the pupils; thirdly, should impart to the study itself of practical work the character of a sound systematical acquirement of knowledge; and fourthly, and lastly, as should facilitate the demonstration of the progress of every pupil at every stated time.[28]

Della Vos and his staff had developed a system of manual instruction in which: (1) each trade such as carpentry, joinery and metal forging was assigned an instruction shop of its own; (2) each shop was assigned with as many working places and sets of tools as there were students; (3) exercises done by the students were arranged in a hierarchy of difficulty progressing from the simple to the complex; (4) all work was made from designs and drawings instead of models; (5) drawings used by the advanced students in the program were made by the elementary class in drawing and design; (6) no student could begin a new model or project until he finished whatever he had been working on in a way that was acceptable to the instructor; (7) the grading of work became more difficult as the student progressed in his studies; and (8) every teacher instructing in a specialized area was an expert in that area.[29]

The exhibit of the Russian Imperial Technical Institute in Machinery Hall at the Centennial. Courtesy of the Free Library of Philadelphia.

The course of study at the Imperial Technical School took three years to complete.[30] Its potential for American schools was immediately recognized by educators visiting the Centennial Exhibition. John D. Runkle, president of the Massachusetts Institute of Technology, recalled how:

> At Philadelphia, in 1876, almost the first thing I saw was a small case containing three series of models—one of chipping and filing, one of forging, and one of machine tool work. I saw at once that they were not parts of machines, but simply graded models for teaching manipulations in those arts. In an instant, the problem I had been seeking to solve was clear to my mind; a plain distinction between a mechanic art and its application in some special trade became apparent.[31]

Runkle's reaction to the Russian exhibit was precisely the sort of response Della Vos had hoped to receive from educators visiting the Centennial. According to Della Vos:

> Everything that we have exhibited at the international exhibition...was exhibited in the desire of sharing with specialists in the work of technical education in the New World all those results that have been attained by the school ....[32]

Immediately on his return from the Centennial Exposition, Runkle suggested that the Massachusetts Institute of Technology establish a training program similar to the one he saw exhibited by the Russians at Philadelphia. On August 17, 1876, a shopwork department was established by the Institute. The department was established and its courses provided training for students in mechancal engineering and was open to other students at the Institute on an elective basis. A new secondary school, using the Russian curriculum, the "School of Mechanic Arts," was established in order to provide younger students with training in industrial education.[33]

Runkle began to promote the Russian system among educators in Massachusetts. In an article included in the Forty-First Annual Report of the Massachusetts Board of Education he outlined in detail the philosophy and purpose of the Russian system:

> Making the art and not the trade fundamental, and then teaching the art by purely educational methods, is the Russian system. The system is instruction in the arts for the purpose of instruction and not construction for the purpose of instruction. The method is not only educational, but it constitutes the only true and philosophical key to all industrial education.[34]

Runkle argued that the system of manual training developed by the Russians represented the key to fulfilling the needs of modern industry.

> If we can formulate into an educational method the arts which apply in any particular industry, we have only to group about these art courses such other subjects of study as obviously pertain to this industry to have a scheme which shall most surely and directly fit the student both in theory and practice upon its pursuit.[35]

Runkle's ideas concerning the application of the Russian system to the American schools were received with a great deal of enthusiasm. Responding to a presentation by him at the National Education Association Meeting in 1877, Dr. Buchanan of Louisville exclaimed:

> While industrial education thus becomes an assistant to intellectual growth and mental discipline, it is destined to revolutionize the world in its social condition, and that revolution is now beginning. It will certainly double the produc-

tive power of more than a million laborers. If it makes these laborers (now worth a dollar a day) worth two or three it will do more to elevate our population in the social scale, increase the general propensity and terminate the conflict of capital and labor than any agency now in the field of progress.[36]

In doing so, the mechanical and industrial arts would have their social status elevated, their productive power increased, and in time make possible a "new industrial world."[37]

While Runkle was the first American educator to call attention to and use the Russian system, it was Calvin M. Woodward of Washington University, St. Louis, Missouri, who most successfully promoted its use in the schools. A New Englander educated at Harvard, Woodward had become a member of the Washington University faculty in 1865. In 1866 he also became associated with the O'Fallon Polytechnic Institute, an evening school that provided instruction for apprentices and journeymen. Two years later he was authorized to establish an engineering department in conjunction with the university.[38]

Technical and design drawing was a topic that was widely emphasized in many of the exhibits at the Centennial Exhibition, as can be seen in this photograph of exhibit materials from France. Courtesy of the Free Library of Philadelphia.

Woodward found it necessary to provide his students at the Polytechnic Institute with training in woodworking and other manual skills. Their inability to use the most simple hand tools made it impossible for them to construct the basic models for his Applied Mechanics class. Feeling that their inexperience was a result of the failure of their schooling, and the fact that they were raised in largely urban environments, Woodward had spent the years prior to the Exposition experimenting with various curriculums that would provide instruction in the manual and industrial arts.[39]

Woodward learned of Runkle's work with the Russian system in 1877, and at that time presented the curriculum to the Board of Trustees at Washington University. On June 6, 1879, the Manual Training School of Washington University was officially established. Commonly recognized as the first manual training school in the United States, it provided a three-year secondary curriculum in which mathematics, drawing, science, languages, history and literature were combined with instruction in woodworking, wood-turning, pattern-making, forging, and so on. Through Runkle, Woodward had esentially adopted the Russian system in its entirety.[40]

It was as a result of Woodward and his work at Washington University that the Russian or Della Vos system came to be the primary model for manual and industrial training in the United States during the 1880s. By means of the Centennial Exhibition, an innovative European curriculum had been introduced into the schools—one which was to have a profound influence on American education.

Closely related to the displays of technical and industrial schools at the Centennial Exhibition were the exhibits of technical drawing vs "art work and drawing" from various schools throughout the country. Interest in art education at the expositions began with the London Crystal Palace Exhibition in 1851. As a result of the displays, the South Kensington. or as it was later known, the Victoria and Albert Museum, was established shortly after the Exhibition and rapidly became the center for instruction in design and drawing during the second half of the nineteenth century.

The Crystal Palace Exhibition had forced the English to recognize the inferiority of their manufacturing designs, and to develop programs in art instruction. By the time of the Centennial Exhibition, according to observers from the period, it was clear that England had become preeminent in industrial design and arts, and that the United States had fallen behind. As Walter Smith, the art director for the state of Massachusetts explained in a speech to the Massachusetts Teachers' Association in 1878:

No thoughtful American can have examined the two great exhibitions at Philadelphia and Paris, as I have done, without feeling that this country does not show well at such displays in comparison with many European countries. It used to be the monopoly of England to stand lowest in the visible evidences of civilization, as seen in her manufacturing industries. I am sorry to be obliged to say that to-day we in America have inherited that reputation which England has lost.[41]

The realization of the need for art instruction in the public schools had clearly been realized in states such as Massachusetts as early as the late 1860s. Rather than the pursuit of art for its own sake, skills such as drawing were promoted because they served the needs of industry. The promotion of art in the schools was seen as leading to improvements in industrial design and manufacture. As the Unitarian leader, Reverend Edward Everett Hale explained during the late 1860s:

> It will be impossible for Massachusetts to maintain any eminence in the higher manufactures if the great body of workmen of other countries are the superiors to our own in the arts of design, in the drafting of machinery, and in the habits of observation which spring from such accomplishments. It is already [said?] by manufacturers here that for any processes which involve a knowledge of the arts of design that they are almost always obliged to engage Englishmen, Frenchmen, Belgians, Germans or Italians.[42]

Similar views were repeated a few years later by visitors to the Centennial Exhibition. Numerous American educators visiting the Centennial Exhibition argued that the introduction of technical and industrial drawing into the public schools would eventually produce a revolution in American manufacturing and industry. As William Torrey Harris explained:

> It is a strange thought that this simple change in the course of study of our common schools, making industrial drawing a regular branch of study, and laying a great stress upon it, will be sufficient after a few years, to modify the national character.[43]

The foundation for a new American industrial order would be established—one which would eventually dominate world culture and economy.[44]

Harris's comments suggest an interesting perception of the equation that knowledge is power. Through the development of superior industrial methods and techniques, the United States would hold an increasingly powerful position in world affairs. Innovation in industry would to a large degree be dependent upon educating individuals to work in an industrial context—one which would demand new skills and new approaches to problems.

The educational exhibit from Massachusetts strongly promoted the concept of industrial development being supported by the establishment of art education programs in the public schools. This was consistent with the policy state educational officials had been supporting for a number of years. As early as 1868 laws had been passed by state legislature which encouraged local school systems to set up art programs. Further legislation was passed in 1870 requiring that all cities and towns with populations of more than ten thousand people provide free instruction in industrial drawing to anyone over the age of fifteen who was interested in having lessons. At the same time, the position of State Director of Art Education was created in order to supervise programs in art instruction throughout the state.[45]

At the Centennial Exposition a total of two-hundred and forty-one framed pictures, fifty portfolios and numerous drawers of drawings were included as part of the Massachusetts exhibit. Geometrical and technical drawings dominated. The character and scope of the art exhibit is clearly conveyed in a description by a reporter for the *Chicago Tribune*:

The Massachusetts State Building. Courtesy of the Free Library of Philadelphia.

I strolled to the eastern end of the great hall and looked at the Massachusetts exhibit, which was there displayed. There were many things there of interest, but what most attracted my attention was the section devoted to drawing and designing ...The instruction is of the most systematic character; it begins with making a dot on a line, and ends I don't know exactly where. At first the pupil works from a flat copy; then he draws from an object; he learns how to make outlines and shades; he copies from houses, animals, machinery, furniture—anything everything; and he is instructed in various technical things until he is ready to enter the higher schools of technology.[46]

Although Massachusetts's art exhibit was the most extensive display of its type at the Centennial, many other states and foreign exhibitors included drawings and other types of art work. New Jersey included over one thousand unframed drawings and over one hundred framed works as part of their state exhibit.[47] Similar displays of art were included in the English exhibit, the exhibit from the province of Ontario, the St. Louis school exhibit and the New York, Ohio, and Rhode Island displays.[48]

The impact that the exhibits had in general on visitors to the Centennial who were not educators is difficult to accurately assess. In the case of art education, the numerous articles describing the various foreign and state exhibits published in newspapers and popular magazines at the time suggest widespread interest in the subject.[49] In examining the foreign, state and local educational exhibits in general, one is immediately impressed by the number of exhibitors, as well as by their scope and size. Foreign educational exhibits were mounted by England, Hawaii, Egypt, Denmark, Sweden, Italy, Brazil, the Netherlands, Belgium, Switzerland, Austria, Germany, France, Canada, Russia and Japan. Major state exhibits were presented by Massachusetts, Pennsylvania, Illinois, Michigan, Wisconsin, New Hampshire, Maryland, Kentucky, Ohio, Indiana, Missouri, Iowa, Maine, Rhode Island, New Jersey and Connecticut. Local school systems such as St. Louis included major exhibits, as did private institutions such as the Stevens Institute of Technology, the Worcester Free Institute, Cornell University and others.[50]

The exhaustive nature of the educational exhibits is typified by the Missouri School Exhibit. A total of one hundred and forty-nine volumes of materials were sent to the Centennial for exhibit. Included among these volumes were examples of school papers from grammer schools throughout the state in subjects such as Arithmetic, English, Grammar, Geography, Natural Science and History. Specimens of German penmanship, examples of drawing, photographs of school buildings, examples of kindergarten work, complete sets of annual school board reports for the city of St. Louis, annual reports from the state university, photographs of Washington University and Mary Institute, as well as examination papers from different public schools and colleges and universities were included in the exhibit.[51]

Gamble School, Exhibit of the St. Louis Public Schools Philadelphia Centennial Exhibition. Personal collection of author.

Colored School Number 2. Exhibit of the St. Louis Public Schools Philadelphia Centennial Exhibition. Personal collection of author.

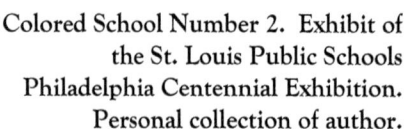

Dodier School, exhibit of the St. Louis Public Schools Philadelphia Centennial Exhibition. Personal collection of author.

Charles Pope School, exhibit of the St. Louis Public Schools Philadelphia Centennial Exhibition. Personal collection of author.

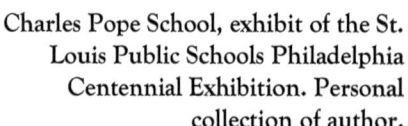

Many of the original volumes and portfolios exhibited by the St. Louis Public Schools as part of the Missouri educational exhibit have been preserved.[52] In examining them, one is immediately overwhelmed by their sheer volume. Thousands of pages of classroom work, drawings, photographs, annual reports and statistical summaries made up the volumes sent to the Centennial. No matter how conscientious or interested a visitor might have been it would have been impossible to carefully examine everything that was on display.

It is clear that the foreign, state and local educational exhibits were intended to be comprehensive in nature. In describing the Ontario educational exhibit, J. George Hodgins explained:

> ...the Exhibit was so planned and furnished that a stranger, if he should be able to devote time to a careful study of the abundant information and material placed before him, would without difficulty understand the whole structure and policy of our educational system,—its history, progress and development, and the means employed for making it effective for the purposes which it was designed to serve in its establishment.[53]

In acting in this way, the educational exhibits provided the means by which foreign and American educators could compare the curriculums and administrations of educational institutions throughout the world. The most advanced pedagogical techniques and methods of each nation were displayed. Equally important, educators from around the world were brought together to exchange information and ideas.

In assembling exhibits for the educational displays educators were forced to carefully assess the organization and procedures of their school systems. In doing so, many educators both in the United States and abroad were forced to ask themselves how good their schools actually were. Issues of national, as well as state and local pride clearly came into play. With American exhibitors, for example, the desire to assemble comprehensive and informative exhibits was also linked to what was an obvious desire to demonstrate the superiority of American education. Prior to the opening of the Centennial Exposition, J. P. Wickersham, the Superintendent of Schools for Pennsylvania, was not alone among American educators in coming to the conclusion that American educators in coming to the conclusion that American schools might not be equal to their European counterparts.[54] Underneath their boisterous enthusiasm for their schools many American educators elicited a profound disquiet. Commenting on the failure of the educational exhibits at the

Centennial to catch the attention of the general public, H. F. Harrison argued that this lack of interest when:

> ...set over against the vaunting pretentions of the people on the subject of education, discrediting those pretentions through the force of the shameful contrast, they acquire a momentous significance. I am led to associate with them the further striking fact, that there are vital points as to which the working of American common schools in general has long been radically defective, subverting their true purposes or crippling their efficiency; and yet, that, with all the boastful pretentions prevalent in regard to them, there is no alarm abroad, no spirit of reform. And I cannot avoid the conclusion that there is something hollow and unreal about the attitude of the American people on the subject of their common-school system.[55]

Harrison's comments were not necessarily borne out. Within the actual educational exhibits themselves at the Centennial Exhibition the vitality of American schooling during the period is clearly evident. This is particularly the case with the model kindergarten, which was among the most popular of the educational exhibits at the Centennial Exhibition.

The American Kindergarten Building at the Philadelphia Centennial Exhibition. Courtesy of the Free Library of Philadelphia.

Although interest in kindergarten education in the United States dates back to the mid-1950s, widespread public acceptance of the kindergartens did not begin until nearly two decades later.[56] Basing their work upon the pioneering efforts of Elizabeth Palmer Peabody and Maria Kraus-Boelte, Susan Blow a young St. Louis socialite, and William Torrey Harris, the superintendent of schools, began the first successful public kindergartens in the United States in St. Louis in the fall of 1873.[57]

The Des Peres kindergarten, 1873. One of the photographs included as part of the St. Louis School Exhibit at the Philadelphia Centennial Exhibition. Personal collection of author.

Despite the success of the kindergartens in St. Louis, public interest and support for them developed gradually. It was not, in fact, at the Centennial Exhibition that Froebel's ideas were brought to the general attention of the American public. Interestingly, Philadelphia was not the first exposition in which kindergarten materials were placed on display. Handbooks, and other didactic materials, had consistently been displayed by manufacturers at expositions in Europe beginning as early as 1854. Yet many individuals seem to have felt that the exhibits of materials at the expositions had done more harm than good for the kindergarten cause. Emphasizing that kindergarten education involved a process as much as a specific set of materials, kindergarten leaders such as Elizabeth Peabody and Milton Bradley argued that the only way to demonstrate the kindergarten process at the Centennial Exhibition would be to include as part of the exhibit an actual working kindergarten, rather than just teaching materials.[58]

Under the sponsorship of the Women's Committee, it was proposed that a kindergarten demonstration class be organized. Space for the kindergarten was promised by the Centennial's officials, while the New York publisher E. Steiger agreed to provide the books, equipment and other educational materials necessary to run the class.[59] Funds to provide the salary for an instructor were solicited from various educational organizations and charitable groups.[60]

An illustration of Froebel's Tenth Gift, "Peas and Globes," a construction toy that evolved into today's "Tinkertoys," which was included as part of the Kindergarten materials displayed by the Milton Bradley Company at the Philadelphia Centennial Exhibition.

In the fall of 1875, Miss Ruth R. Burritt came to Philadelphia at the request of Elizabeth Peabody and Frances McDaniel.[61] Burritt was an experienced kindergartener and well suited for the job. Originally trained by Elizabeth Peabody, Miss Burritt had been working for a number of years in schools in Wisconson.[62]

Once Miss Burritt was selected as the instructor, arrangements were made with an orphanage, the Northern Home for Friendless Children, to provide the students needed for the demonstration class. Burritt began instructing the children selected at the orphanage in October of 1875. On May 15, 1876, the children were brought to the Exposition for the first time to begin the demonstration classes.[63] From May 15th to October 15th demonstration classes were held from 10:00 am to 12:30 pm every Monday, Tuesday and Wednesday.[64]

The demonstration kindergarten was held in a modest one-room building constructed specifically for the use of Miss Burritt and her class. When classes were not in session, it was possible for visitors to the exhibit to carefully examine the materials used in the instruction of the children. In addition to the demonstration kindergarten and its displays, visitors were able to see various kindergarten materials included in the state and local exhibits.

The Philadelphia Centennial Exhibition

Children being taught in the Kindergarten Cottage at the Philadelphia Centennial Exhibition, *Frank Leslies Historical Register of the United States Centennial Exposition,* 1876, edited by Frank H. Norton (New York: Frank Leslie's Publishing Company, 1877), p. 118.

One of the visitors to these exhibits was Mrs. William Wright of Weymouth, Massachusetts, the mother of the architect Frank Lloyd Wright. In a remarkable section of his autobiography, Frank Lloyd Wright recalls how:

> At the Centennial in Philadelphia, after a sightseeing day, mother made a discovery ...The kindergarten! She had seen the "Gifts" in the Exposition Building. The strips of colored paper, glazed and "matt," remarkably soft brilliant colors. Now came the geometric by-play of those charming checkered combinations! The structural digures to be made with peas and globes. The smooth shapely maple blocks with which to build, the sense of which never afterward leaves the fingers: *form* becoming *feeling.*[65]

After her return from Philadelphia, Wright's mother purchased a set of the Frobelian Gifts to use with her children. Their use was to have a profound effect upon her son. Recounting his experience with the kindergarten materials many years later Wright explained how:

> A small interior world of color and form now came within grasp of small fingers. Color and pattern, in the flat, in the round. Shapes that lay hidden behind the appearances all about ...Here was something for invention to seize,

and use to create. These "Gifts" came into the gray house in drab old Weymouth and made something live that had never lived before.[66]

The probable influence of Froebel's Gifts on Wright's work as an architect has been carefully analyzed by scholars.[67] Yet his introduction to the Froebelian materials as a result of the Centennial Exposition was most certainly not a unique experience. During the six months in which the Centennial Exposition was held in Fairmont Park, thousands of people like Mrs. Wright must have seen and been impresssed by the kindergarten exhibits.[68]

Although the main focus of the Centennial kindergarten exhibits was the demonstration kindergarten, other important kindergarten displays were included as well. In the Massachusetts exhibit the work of kindergarten children between the ages of four and six was displayed, as well as materials from Milton Bradley and Company.[69] Materials were also exhibited in the U.S. Government Building, as well as in the Pennsylvania and Ontario exhibits. Of particular interest was the kindergarten exhibit included as part of the Missouri exhibit. Assembled under the supervision of the pioneer kindergarten educator Susan Blow was an extensive display of work done by the children in the public kindergartens in St. Louis. The unusual quality of the work included in the exhibit was commented upon by Elizabeth Peabody:

> I found the children's inventions in weaving, pricking, sewing, folding, cutting, etc., were arranged in books; and looking over them, I was struck by the variety of the inventions, which proved what I have heard said of Miss Blows's power to inspire and encourage originality.[70]

Separate from the Missouri kindergarten exhibit was the display of the St. Louis public schools in which were included a remarkable collection of photographs of the public kindergartens in St. Louis.

Educators paying careful attention to the printed materials included in the Missouri educational exhibit would find a great deal to study and reflect upon in terms of kindergarten education. Included, for example, as part of the Annual Report for the St. Louis Public Schools were detailed descriptions of the establishment and operation of the kindergarten under Miss Blow. These reports, combined with the actual demonstration kindergarten of Miss Burritt, as well as other exhibits, and the pedagogical materials from the St. Louis public kindergartens, provided an extensive introduction not only to the curriculum and methods of kindergarten education, but also to the practical problems involved with the establishment of kindergartens.

An outdoor garden at the the Des Peres kindergarten. One of the photographs included as part of the St. Louis School Exhibit at the Philadelphia Centennial Exhibition. Personal collection of author.

The Pennsylvania Educational Building. Courtesy of the Free Library of Philadelphia.

In general, the educational exhibits of the various states followed a pattern similar to that described for Missouri. A total of thirteen states (including Missouri) mounted educational exhibits. These included Pennsylvania, Massachusetts, Ohio, New Jersey, Connecticut, Rhode Island, New Hampshire, Maine, Illinois, Indiana, Michigan, and Wisconsin. Undoubtedly, the most extensive of these exhibits was from Pennsylvania.

The Pennsylvania educational exhibit was housed in a separate octagonal building that included over 20, 000 square feet of wall surface for exhibitors. Included in the building were exhibits relating to kinderagarten education, progress in the design of school equipment between 1776 and 1876, the education of the blind, orphan schools, etc. As in the case of the Missouri educational exhibit, various state and local publications relating to the schools, as well as examples of work done by students were included in the exhibits.[71]

In general, there seems to have been a high degree of uniformity in the content of the educational exhibits between the various states. This is despite the fact that educational systems in each of these states were under the control of independent local Boards of Education separate from the Federal Government. As will subsequently be seen in this study, this tendency towards a relatively uniform system of schools throughout the country becomes even more pronounced at the succeeding expositions in Chicago and St. Louis.

In examining the educational exhibits of the various states at the Philadelphia Centennial Exhibition, it is important to recognize that those states with educational exhibits were by no means representative of the entire country. All of the states which included educational exhibits were located in either the Northeast or the Midwest.

It was on an international basis that the Centennial Exhibition was particularly important for American educators. By bringing together people and exhibits from around the world, the Centennial forced American educators to critically consider both new pedagogical ideas and the effectiveness of existing educational programs. In an era when opportunities for contacts between international educators were relatively limited, such a function was extremely important. Undoubtedly, the International Conference on Education that was held in conjunction with the exposition beginning on July 18, 1876 facilitated such international educational contacts.

The International Conference on Education was organized in late June of 1876 as an informal two-day meeting of the major educators visiting the Centennial Exhibition.[72] It included presentations on an incredibly wide range of topics by many speakers. Topics included discussions of teaching conditions in the United States, the development of museums of industrial education, pedagogical museums, conditions of education in Japan, and so on. Virtually all of the foreign educational commissioners made presentations, while leading American educators such as William Torrey Harris, John W. Hoyt, and John Eaton presented papers as well.[73]

The significance of the conference probably lies not so much in the topics that were discussed, but instead in the fact that the conference brought together educational figures in immediate contact with one another and with innovations and educational experiments exhibited as part of the Centennial Exhibition. In examining the minutes from the educational conference it is possible not only to discover what were the current interests of educators from the period, but also to note the beginnings of statistical research in education. Included, for example, at the beginning of the proceedings for the educational conference is a discussion on the significance of compiling educational statistics on an international basis. Implicit in the statement is a fundamental faith in the ability of such information to provide the basis for educational advancement and progress:

> Educational statistics alone can show the way out of the bewildering [types] of different educational systems. They will be of more than ordinary importance in a state occupied with a reforming of its educational system; all such reforms would build on a very unsafe foundation if they had not been preceded and were not constantly accompanied by exhaustive educational statistics.[74]

Essentially, what is being recognized is the need to organize knowledge in new ways. In doing so, the power to redefine the educational system through the organization of knowledge is made possible.

Recognition of the need to develop new ways of organizing and disseminating knowledge was particularly evident in the library exhibits and conferences held in conjunction with the Centennial Exhibition. Included as one of the main exhibits of the United States Bureau of Education was a two-volume report on the *Public Libraries in the United States*.[75] Prepared by Samuel Warren and S. M. Clark at the request of John Eaton, the report represented the most comprehensive analysis of American library history and organization ever undertaken. Volume one contained 1,187 pages and largely dealt with historical and organizational aspects of library work. Volume two, which was 89 pages in length, contained the rules for making a Dictionary Catalogue by Charles A. Cutter, the librarian of the Boston Athenaeum. Of particular interest, in terms of the subsequent development of libraries in the United States was the inclusion in the report of an essay by Melvil Dewey entitled "a Decimal Classification and Subject Index."[76]

Dewey's interest in libraries began in 1872 when he was an undergraduate student at Amherst College. Working as an assistant in the college library, he began to read about library organization and to visit different libraries in New York and New England.[77] Dewey's main concern was how to develop a more efficient cataloguing system than those currently in use. As Dewey explained some years later in an article published in the *Library Journal*:

> In visiting over fifty libraries, I was astounded to find the lack of efficiency, and waste of time and money in constant recataloguing and reclassifying made necessary by the almost universally fixt system where a book was numbered according to the particular room, tier and shelf where it chanced to stand on that day, instead of by class, to which it belonged yesterday, today and forever...[78]

Dewey was directly addressing the question of how to develop more efficient systems of organizing printed information and knowledge. While idiosyncratic means of cataloguing and indexing had been adequate to meet the needs of most libraries durng the first century of the country's history, such methods were becoming increasingly obsolete as more and more printed information in the form of books, pamphlets and periodicals became available. Efficient access to knowledge was a key issue in the development of the increasingly industrialized culture that was coming into existence in the United States by the time of the Centennial Exhibition in 1876.

Dewey's solution of how to organize and catalogue libraries came to him while he was attending chapel one day at Amherst College. Listening to a long sermon by President Stearns, the solution to the cataloguing problem flashed over him and he jumped in his seat

> ...and came very near shouting "Eureka!" It was to get absolute simplicity by using the simplest known symbols, the arabic numerals as decimals with the ordinary significance of nought, to number a classification of all human knowledge in print.[79]

In retrospect, Dewey's classification system seems remarkably simple. Yet in its own way, the Dewey Decimal System represented a major breakthrough in the development of new ways of organizing knowledge and information. The system was presented to the Library Committee at Amherst in the form of a memorandudm in May of 1873 in which the basic principles of the cataloguing system were described, The system was quickly accepted and subsequently published in the report on libraries prepared by the United States Bureau of Education for the Centennial Exhibition. Describing his use of the Decimal System at the Amherst Library, Dewey explained that:

The library is first divided into nine special libraries, which are called classes. These classes are (1) Philosophy, (2) Theology, (3) Sociology, (4) Philology, (5) Natural Science, (6) Useful Arts, (7) Fine Arts, (8) Literature, and (9) History, and are numbered with nine digits; thus Class 9 is the Library of History, etc. These special libraries or classes are then considered independently, and each one is separated again into nine divisions of the main subject. These divisions are numbered from 1 to 9, as were the classes. Thus 59 is the ninth division (Zoology) of the fifth class, (Natural Science).[80]

Dewey had realized a cataloguing system going from zero to 999.999 that would allow the classification and organization of all the world's printed knowledge.

Dewey took advantage of the Centennial to promote and organize support for various causes that he was interested in. Besides providing the means by which to introduce his decimal system on an international basis, the Centennial provided him a means of promoting library, spelling, and metric reform. Clearly something of an intellectual entrepeneur, Dewey recalled how in six months in 1876 he "…had organized three national educational societies …utilizing …the Centennial to hold three national conventions and thus start work."[81]

Significantly, the three areas of reform that Dewey supported represented tendencies towards standardization and efficiency. One of them, metric reform, was widely discusses at the Centennial Exhibition. In the 1877 report of B. G. Northrup, Secretary of the Board of Education for Connecticut, there is a detailed discussion of the metric system. According to Northrup, the Exhibition had

> …given a new illustration of the importance of teaching the metric system in American schools…
>
> By the advance of civilization and the closer relations and growing intercourse which commerce and international expositions are creating among all nations, the metric system is sure to become universal. Our youth should no longer be ignorant of this world language, already in use by the great majority of cultivated nations, and which computing only by decimals, is the most simple and uniform.[82]

Northrup's discussion of the potential use of the metric system by American manufacturers to expand international markets was consistent with his belief that the United States was entering into a new era of trade with countries such as China and Japan. Through education, he believed the United States would lead both of these countries toward a higher level of civilization, and endow them with a new type of power. For Northrup, trade with countries such as China was crucial to future American prosperity.

Specimen Pages of Classification for the Dewey Decimal System included in *Public Libraries of the United States*, Part I (Washington: Government Printing Office, 1876). p. 643.

Our commercial intercourse with China, already great, is rapidly growing. The new demand there for American cottons is one of many illustrations of its growing importance. America cannot afford to alienate China. In no other direction is there such room for the expansion of trade and commerce as with China and Japan. Our nearest neighbors across the Pacific, they may contribute immensely to our prosperity.[83]

By drawing China into a Western educational system, the country would in turn be drawn into trade and commerce which could prove to be of critical importance to the United States in generations to come.

Northrup's belief that Western education and commerce would colonize and civilize much of the world also had important implications for the increasing adoption and use of English as a universal language:

Commerce as well as colonization is a grand propagandist of language. The Saxon tongue is domiciled in every center of trade. Wherever floats a Saxon keel there floats with it Saxon words and commercial terms.[84]

For Northrup, one of the most important functions of the Centennial Exposition was that it made foreign visitors aware of the achievements of industrialized nations such as the United States, and encouraged them to adopt Western values.

The Americanization of various cultures was not limited to just foreign countries. As indicated by the Indian education exhibits included as part of the display of the United States Bureau of Education, "progress" was beginning to have its impact on Native American groups. A correspondent from the New York *Tribune* writing about the exhibit of the Bureau of Education, described how:

> The schools of the Indian Territory have made a very creditable display. They have sent photographs of their school-houses, prominent teachers, and specimens of text-books, chirography, needlework, drawing, etc. The wonderful progress which even some of the wilder tribes of Indians have made in a few years' residence in the Indian Territory as shown in this exhibit, demonstrates the wisdom of an Indian policy that removes the savages from the demoralizing influence of frontier settlements, and places them under direct civilizing influences. The Modocs, even, who a few years ago, from their fastnesses in the lava beds, defied the power of the United States, and spread terror throughout a whole region, are now rapidly learning the arts of civilization, and their schools make a very creditable display in the Centennial Exhibition.[85]

A. Tolman Smith, in writing about the Indian Education Exhibit, also emphasized the idea of the various Indian peoples progressing toward a higher plane of civilization. Smith, for example, quotes a Pawnee by the name of Running Chief to the effect that:

> Following the plow will give me that *active* exercise which I used to get on the hunt; formerly the only way for a Pawnee chief to make his mark was to kill a good many of his enemies; to-day the only way is to become a great farmer, a great mechanic, or perhaps a great lawyer.[86]

Whether Native American or Asiatic, education was perceived by the American organizers and participants at the Centennial Exhibition as leading them toward a higher level of civilization.

Smithsonian exhibit of American Indian, artifacts in the United States Government Building at the 1876 Centennial Exhibition. Courtesy of the Smithsonian Institution.

Extensive exhibits were mounted by both China and Japan at the Centennial Exhibition. Japan in particular focused on its educational exhibit. Earlier international expositions had played an important part in Japan's modernization process.[87] In 1873, for example, a major science and industry museum was begun with materials brought back to Japan from the international exposition in Vienna. An educational museum was also begun at the same time. Materials from this source provided the nucleus for the Japanese educational exhibit at the Centennial.

Over one thousand objects were included in the Japanese educational exhibit. Textbooks, annual reports of the ministry of education, kindergarten materials, devices for the teaching of the physical sciences, photographs of schools and libraries, curricula and newspapers, are examples of just a few of the items that made up the exhibit.[88]

The Pennsylvania Educational Building. Courtesy of the Free Library of Philadelphia.

As was the case at Vienna in 1873, Japan acquired many educational items from various foreign exhibits, once the exposition was over. In exchange for materials such as photographs of Japanese schools and examples of Japanese students' work, Japan obtained an enormous collection of photographs, scientific apparatus and books from the Ontario Department of Education.[89]

Nearly all of the educational materials exchanged between various foreign countries were intended to be used as exhibits for pedagogical and educational museums. Interest in pedagogical museums at the Centennial Exhibition had been stimulated to a large degree by the exhibit of the Pedagogic Museum of St. Petersburg. Begun in 1864, the St. Petersburg Pedagogic Museum was established with the idea of collecting and diffusing:

> ...information in regard to the best school apparatus made in Russia or abroad, and to exhibit the fullest possible collection of the same, so as to facilitate selection and purchase to suit individual requirements.[90]

While at the Centennial Exhibition, Russian delegates carefully collected materials on various American and foreign educational exhibits. Catalogues of materials were compiled, various apparatus, books and specimens were obtained and sent back to Russia and the Pedagogic Museum in St. Petersburg.[91]

The Ontario Exhibit at the Philadelphia Centennial Exhibition. Courtesy of the Free Library of Philadelphia.

Russian educational materials from the Pedagogic Museum at St. Petersburg on display at the Centennial Exhibition. Courtesy of the Free Library of Philadelphia.

Other educational museums, including the Pedagogical Museum of Vienna, the Pedagogical Department of the South Kensington Museum of London and the Industrial Museum of Zurich, displayed materials at Philadelphia. Together with the St. Petersburg Pedagogic Museum, the museum exhibits at the Centennial Exhibition provided a major stimulus for museum development in both Europe and America.

In the case of the United States, the Exposition played a particularly important role in museum development. Following the Centennial Exposition, many of the foreign exhibitors contributed their materials to the Smithsonian Institution in Washington, D.C. These contributions, together with the special efforts made by the Smithsonian in assembling exhibits for the Centennial Exposition, provided an important impetus for the expansion and development of the National Museum in Washington.

At the Centennial Exposition, the Smithsonian Institution was responsible for a wide-range of government exhibits. The Smithsonian itself sent a complete collection of all the publications of the Institution, as well as exhibits concerning international exchanges of scientific materials and information about the climate and geography of the United States. The National Museum, under the direction of the Smithsonian Institution, mounted exhibits on the mineral wealth of the United States and its plants and animals. Of particular interest to many of the visitors to the Centennial Exhibition were the plaster and papier-mâché models of fish and crustaceans that were put together by the Smithsonian and the United States Fish Commission.[92] Professor Archer, one of the English commissioners to the Exhibition described the Smithsonian exhibits that were housed in the U.S. Government Building as follows:

> Within the chief building was displayed most interesting and instructive collections, illustrative of the work of the Smithsonian Institution, and the general and geological surveys of the States, the mineral, zoological, and botanical collections collected with those surveys, and also most important ethnological and prehistoric collections. The great collections of food-fishes of America, made for the Fishery Commission by Professor Baird, with the appliances for catching and preserving fish; also series illustrating the various naval and military weapons and engines, and machinery for arsenal work; and, lastly, a compete display of all the applications in the postal department of the states. The general arrangement of the contents of this large building, covering about two acres, was most satisfactory and had been carried out under the most competent scientific supervision, hence it was felt to be a most instructive portion of the Centennial Exhibition. It brought into full view a great mass of the intellectual work of some of the greatest of American workers in the fields of science.[93]

A total of approximately 34, 000 square feet of exhibit space was occupied by the collections of the National Museum, taking up about forty-one percent of the total exhibit space of the Government Building.[94] This was nearly double the capacity of the Smithsonian's own building in Washington, D.C.

Since it had always been the intention of the government to return the exhibits from the Centennial Exhibition to Washington to be incorporated into the collection of the National Museum, a serious space problem had been created.

The shortage of space for the Smithsonian caused by the new displays prepared for the United States Government Exhibit was further compounded by the gift of exhibit materials from various foreign groups. Collections were received from the Argentine Republic, Austria, the Orange Free State, Belgium, Brazil, Chile, China, Egypt, France, the German Empire, the Hawaiian Islands, Japan, Mexico, the Netherlands, Norway, Peru, Portugal, Russia, Spain, the Phillipines, Sweden, Switzerland, Tunis, Turkey, the United Kingdom, Bermuda, Canada, New South Wales, New Zealand, Queensland, South Australia, Tasmania, Victoria and Venezuela.[95] Over fifty large freight cars were eventually sent back to the National Museum in Washington, D.C.[96]

The fisheries exhibit from the Smithsonian at the Centennial Exhibition was extremely popular.

Realizing the immediate need to provide further exhibition space for the National Museum as a result of the new collections obtained from the Centennial, Congress appropriated $250,000 to build a major extension, known as the "Arts and Industries Building," onto the exhibition hall that has affectionately come to symbolize the Smithsonian, and which is today known as "the Castle."[97] The provision of funds by the Congress in order to expand the Smithsonian reflected a growing awareness of the importance of museums as an educational force. This awareness was clearly encouraged by the positive experience of the Centennial Exhibition. William Sounders, a representative from the Agricultural Department, for example, argued in Congress for the need to expand the facilities of the National Museum. As he explained:

> As to the educational value of museums of natural history, it cannot well be overrated; as a means of diffusing instruction and rational amusement among the people and giving to the scientific student every possible means of practical examination and study of specimens connected with the nature of his researches, museums stand foremost as practical educators; their influence in promoting and extending manufactures and commerce is being appreciated throughout the world; they are the natural offspring of international exhibitions; they are permanent exhibits of the world's progress.[98]

In much the same way that the international expositions were seen as promoting progress through the dissemination of knowledge, permanent museums such as the Smithsonian's Museum would serve the same function.

The theme that knowledge is power, and the relationship between knowledge and progress which so dominated the educational exhibits at the Exhibition was emphasized in a particularly interesting way by the federal Bureau of Education's request prior to the Centennial Exposition, that each state would submit as part of their educational exhibit materials describing not only the current opportunities for education in their regions, but also a history of their development and progress. As mentioned earlier in this chapter, a letter with a synopsis outlining a proposed "Centennial History of American Education" was sent to school superintendents and city and state boards of education.[99] This synopsis was also included in the Commissioner's report for 1875.[100] The proposed format for the Centennial History is very revealing in reference to its author's conception of the role of education in American culture. Three historical periods were outlined: (1) the Colonial Period, (2) the Homogenous Period, (1776-1840), and (3) the Hetrogeneous Period (1840-

1876). In the "Hetrogeneous Period," which covered the time between the establishment of the Common Schools and the Centennial Exhibition, the idea of progress at all levels of schooling, from the elementary through the collegiate levels is emphasized. In fact, the word "progress" is repeated over and over again in the document to such an extent that one cannot help but feel that it, and the concept it defines, was a preoccupation of the authors of the synopsis. Equally revealing is the section outlining "Influences and Results." Near the end of this section we find:

> ...the heterogeneous character of the population since 1846; the character and intelligence of the immigrants; the progress of industries; of agriculture; the development of means for speedy transportation; international literature; the scientific spirit; etcetera.[101]

Progress and education as outlined in the synopsis are part of the same process. Together they are leading the American people toward an increasingly sophisticated technological and industrial society. If power is to be equated with this progress in technology, then following the logic of the synopsis, education is its key.

The significance of the Bureau of Education's synopsis for the "Centennial History of American Education" has been overlooked by contemporary educational historians. Only Lawrence Cremin in his essay *The Wonderful World of Ellwood Patterson Cubberly* recognized that the format for the Synopsis for the Proposed Centennial History

> ...is striking, for it forced the vastly different histories of the several states into a common mold and enabled them for the first time to tell a common story. Out of the "spirit of '76" came the earliest history of American education.[102]

Relatively few state educational histories were in fact written for the Centennial Exhibition.[103] In general, those that were written were dreary documents. often reflecting the fact that they were assembled by committees of writers on very short notice. Short on scholarship, and often anecdotal in nature, the state educational histories did not even come close to providing the foundation for the national history of education proposed by John Eaton and his colleagues in the United States Bureau of Education.

Ironically, rather than the state histories of education themselves, it is the call for papers, and in particular the "Synopsis of the Proposed Centennial History of American Education—1776-1876" that is of greatest significance to the historiography of American education. Essentially the Centennial Synopsis contains the seed for the myth of the public school triumphant—a view developed most completely in the twentieth century by the educator Ellwood P. Cubberly in *Public Education in the United States*.[104]

Cubberly's work and its place in the historiography of American educational history has been carefully analyzed by Lawrence Cremin in *The Wonderful World of Ellwood Patterson Cubberly*.[105] Cubberley's work parallels the Bureau of Education's "Synopsis" to a remarkable degree. In his introduction, for example, Cubberley explains that:

> To be familiar with recent development, to be able to view present-day educational problems in light of their historical evolution and their political and social bearings, and to see educational service in its proper setting as a great national institution evolved by democracy to help solve its perplexing problems, the writer holds to be of fundamental importance to the beginning student of education.[106]

Cubberley then goes on to explain the contents of the book:

> The first chapter gives the European background; the next three describe the establishment of education on our shores, and trace its development through the Colonial and early National periods; the next five treat the half century of struggle to establish education as a function of the state, described the schools established and cover the period up to about 1850;...[107]

Cubberley's outline continues up into the beginning of the twentieth century. As Cremin has explained, "Cubberley shared the progressive vision of the public school as society's chief lever of social improvement. It is not surprising, therefore, that he saw the evolution of the public school as the leitmotif of American Educational History."[108] Bernard Bailyn characterized historians such as Cubberley as having fallen into the trap of interpreting the past as "simply the present writ small."[109] In other words, that the roots of our present culture, and in the case of Cubberley, our educational system, is simply a logical extension or continuation of our European heritage and early Colonial experience.

The Bureau of Education's "Synopsis" presents precisely such an interpretation of American educational history. In the section on secondary education, for example, the Colonial period includes a description of early grammar schools; during the "homogeneous" period from 1776 to 1840, these schools are seen as increasing; and finally during the "hetrogeneous" period, 1840-1876, there is seen the "rise and progress of the free public high schools."[110]

Culture as Curriculum

Synopsis of the proposed ... *History of American education—1776–1876.*

Grade or kind of instruction.	The colonial period.		The homogeneous period—1776–1840.		The heterogeneous period—1840–1876.	
	Educational topics.	Influences and results.	Educational topics.	Influences and results.	Educational topics.	Influences and results.
ELEMENTARY	The early schools in the colonies of Spain, England, France, and Holland briefly noticed; digest of the colonial laws respecting elementary schools; horn books; the New England primer; biographies of early pedagogues, &c.	Positive, habilitations, and attitude of the European nations which colonized North America; supremacy of Spain under Charles I and Philip II. (1516–1598;) of France under Louis XIV. (1658–1714;) of England under Elizabeth and James (1558–1625;) of England under Cromwell, (1648–1660;) of England under Marlborough and Chatham, (1701–1776;) political, social, and religious institutions of the colonists; political and military events in the colonies.	The Virginia territorial cession, and the ordinance of 1787; history of two school land sales and of elementary schools; origin of free schools under State authority; learned men, Mann, Barnard, Sears, Emerson, and others; illiteracy of the country in 1840, &c.; biography and bibliography.	Homogeneity of the population; comparatively small annual immigration, (1775;) Webster's spelling-book, (1783;) the Federal Constitution, (1787;) copyright law, (1790;) naturalization, (1795;) Kentucky, Tennessee, Ohio, Mississippi, Illinois, and Alabama, (1792–1819;) Whitney's cotton gin, (1793;) abolition of the slave trade, (1808;) War of 1812–1815; Fulton's steamer on the Hudson, (1807;) province of Louisiana acquired, (1803;) Florida acquired, (1821;) Oregon country, (1840–1846;) introduction of canals, (1817;) Missouri compromise, (1820;) railroads introduced, (1827;) McCormick's reaper, (1832;) the Seminole war, (1835–1842.)	The progress and present condition of free elementary instruction; official supervision of public schools; improvements in school buildings, furniture, and apparatus; character and number of text books; the school reports of the country since 1840; the financial panic of 1873, and 1879; instruction of the colored people and the Indians; Kindergarten; private elementary instruction.	Introduction of the electric telegraph, (1843;) war with Mexico, (1845–1848;) Texas annexed, (1844;) the newly modified (now) the great Irish famine, (1846;) Mormon emigration to Utah, (1847;) discovery of gold in California, (1848;) emigration to the Pacific coast, (1849;) European revolutions, (1848;) great emigration from Europe, (1848 et seq.;) the Mexican cessions, (1849–1853;) the London World's Fair, (1851;) the Paris Exposition, (1867;) the Franco-German war, (1866;) acquisition of Alaska, (1867;) the Paris Exposition, (1867;) the Franco-German war, (1870;) the Austro-Prussian war, (1866;) the war and the abolition of slavery, (1861–1865;) the Atlantic telegraph, (1858;) the London World's Fair, (1862;) the financial panic of 1873; the Vienna Weltausstellung, (1873;) the heterogeneous character of the population since 1860; the characteristics and intelligence of the immigrants; progress of industries; of agriculture; the development of means for speedy transportation; interchange of industries; of agriculture; the development of means for speedy transportation; interchange of literature; the scientific spirit, &c.
SECONDARY	Early grammar schools, public and incorporate; text books; courses of instruction; biographies, bibliography; the clergy as trainers for college.		... grammar schools, and academies, ... duaries ... architectures; th... aims of instruction; bi... raphies, bibliogr... hy, and statistics.		The progress of grammar schools, academies, and female schools; rise and progress of free public high schools, text books, courses of instruction, apparatus, and architecture; business colleges; bibliography, biographies, and statistics.	
SUPERIOR, i. e., COLLEGIATE AND PROFESSIONAL	Early colonial colleges, (e. g., Harvard, William and Mary's, King's, Dartmouth, Yale, Princeton, &c.;) their foundation by colonial and individual action; discipline, text books, and courses of instruction in the classics, mathematics, theology, &c.; biographies and bibliography; connection of religious denominations with the colleges, &c. Early instruction in the professions, particularly law, and medical; Ames' and Mather's ...		The progress of collegiate instruction; text books and courses of instruction in the classics, mathematics, physics, chemistry, political economy, moral and natural science, &c. Colleges in their denomination and public relations; libraries of colleges; bibliographies, and statistics. The progress of theological, medical, and legal education; rise and progress of normal and scientific training; biography, bibliography, and statistics		The progress and present condition of collegiate training; rise of State universities and of colleges of agriculture and the mechanic arts; rise of colleges for women; text books and courses of instruction in mathematics, astronomy, physics, chemistry, geology, mineralogy, botany, political economy, social science, art, history, &c.; (biography in each case a history of the subject of instruction.) The progress and present condition of instruction in theology, jurisprudence, medicine, dentistry, pharmacy and surgery; rise of military, industrial and collegiate professional training.	
MISCELLANEOUS	Notices of early libraries and of the bibliography of "Americana."		The progress of libraries; rise and progress of museums of science and art; instruction and care of orphans, of the blind, and the deaf mute, &c. Sunday schools. Instruction in art and music. Reformatory and penal instruction. The American Institute of Instruction.		Progress and present condition of libraries, of art museums and science museums; of cheap art schools; instruction of the unfortunate; schools for the feebleminded, &c. Sunday schools. Schools of art and music; cheap reproductions of art works; cheap music; &c. Progress in penology and in reformatory training. Associations for public benefit; churches; societies; the National Bureau of Education.	
ILLUSTRATION	Engravings of early school and college buildings; portraits of educators; maps, &c.		Engravings of school and college buildings, portraits of educators; maps, charts of illiteracy in 1840, &c.		Pictures of buildings for schools, colleges, libraries, museums, asylums, &c.; portraits of teachers and benefactors; maps; illiteracy charts of 1850, 1860, and 1870; diagrams of ventilating apparatus, furniture, &c.	

Cubberley's *Public Education in the United States* not only reflects the myth of the public school triumphant, the basic outline of which can be found in the United States Bureau of Education's "Synopsis of the Proposed Centennial History of American Education—1776-1876," but also in the theme that shows up time and again throughout the educational exhibits at the Centennial Exhibition: that is that knowledge and power are somewhat equated, that education is essential to progress. It is a theme that is picked up by Cubberley at the conclusion of *Public Education in the United States*:

> Education today has become the great constructive tool of civilization. A hundred years ago it was of little importance in the life of a Nation; today it is the prime essential to good government and national progress.[111]

Ultimately, Cubberley's faith in education as a tool of progress represented the continuation of a theme that had begun with the educational exhibits and displays of the 1876 Philadelphia Centennial Exhibition.

* * *

In conclusion, the theme of education as the dynamo or engine of progress in American culture ultimately becomes the main theme of the educational exhibits at the Centennial Exhibition. The idea of education and knowledge as engines of progress is increasingly incorporated into the rhetoric of the educational leaders of the period. Referring to the great Corliss steam engine—the symbol of the Centennial Exhibition—E. E. White, the president of Purdue University wrote in 1881 that the power behind the Corliss engine was " ...a few pounds of imprisoned steam in the great engine of the centre."[112] In much the same way the force of education was seen as the power and engine driving the new industrialized society that was emerging in America by the second half of the nineteenth century. As White explained:

> What the matchless engine in Machinery Hall was to its myriads of mechancical operations, education is to the multiplying forms of human labor. The public school is the Corliss engine of American industry.[113]

Education and industry were inseparable in the scheme of progress and power that had emerged at the Centennial Exhibition.

Notes

1 *International Exhibition, 1876. Reports and Awards Group XXVIII*, Edited by Francis A. Walker (Philadelphia: Lippincott & Co., 1878), pp. 4-5.

2   Ibid., p. 5.
3   Unfortunately most of the correspondence of the United States Commissioner of Education concerning the educational exhibits and congresses held at the exposition in Philadelphia, Chicago and St. Louis has been lost. "Press Copies" of letters sent by John Eaton during 1875 and 1876 included in the National Archive, Washington, D.C. (Microphony #635, rolls number 4–8) indicate that Eaton and the United States Bureau of Education were involved in arranging the assembly and shipping of exhibits from around the country and internationally. Roll number 62 of the same microfilm series includes an extensive correspondence about the educational exhibit held at the World's Industrial and Cotton Centennial Exposition held in New Orleans in 1884. No correspondence of any sort survives from the Commissioners from 1893 or 1904, the years when the expositions were held in Chicago and St. Louis.
4   *International Exhibition 1876. Connecticut in the Department of Education and Science at Philadelphia* (New Haven, CT: B. G. Northrup, December 20, 1875), p. 2.
5   *Annual Report, United States Commissioner of Education* (Washington, DC: United States Government Printing Office, 1874), p. cxxvii.
6   *American Education as Described by the French Commission to the International Exhibition of 1876*, Circular of Information #5–1879, Bureau of Education (Washington, DC: Government Printing Office, 1879), p. 12. This circular is a partial translation of a report by M. Ferdinand Buisson, et al. to the French government entitled *Rapport sur l'instruction primaire a l'exposition universelle de Philadelphie en 1876* (Paris: Imprimerie nationale, 1878).
7   Ibid.
8   For extended discussions of the tradition of the "self-made man" see: Irvin G. Wylier, *The Self-Made Man in America* (New York: The Free Press, 1954); and John G. Cawleti, *Apostles of the Self-Made Man* (Chicago: University of Chicago Press, 1968).
9   *American Education as Described by the French Commissioner to the International Exhibition of 1876*, op. cit., pp. 12–13.
10 B. G. Northrup, "Educational Lessons from the Centennial," *Annual Report of the Board of Education of the State of Connecticut*, January 1877 session (New Haven, CT: Tuttle, Morehouse and Taylor, Printers, 1877), p. 27.
11 Ibid.
12 William Torrey Harris, "The Centennial Exposition," *Twenty-Second Annual Report of the Board of Directors of the St. Louis Public Schools for the Year Ending August 1, 1876* (St. Louis, MO: Slawson, Printer, 1877), p. 173.
13 *International Exhibition, 1876. Reports and Awards Group XXVII*, pp. 2–3.
14 H. F. Harrington, "The Educational Exhibit at Philadelphia," *New England Journal of Education*, 4, no. 98, Dec. 16, 1876, p. 267.

15 Ibid., pp. 267-68.
16 "The Educational Exhibit of Foreign Countries," *Weekly State Gazette*, July 27, 1876.
17 "Sweden at the Centennial," *Scientific American Supplement*, no. 18, April 19, 1876, p. 282.
18 *International Exhibition, 1876. Reports and Awards Groups XXCII*, op. cit., p. 189.
19 Quoted by Hodgins, op. cit., p. 60.
20 Harris, op. cit., p. 176.
21 Ibid., pp. 176-177.
22 Ibid., p. 177.
23 Ibid., p. 178.
24 "Technical Education in the United States as Illustrated at the Centennial," *Scientific American*, 35, no. 5, July 29, 1876, pp. 67-68.
25 Ibid.
26 For a general outline and description of the Russian exhibit see: *Catalogue of the Russian Section, International Exhibition of 1876* (С. НЕТЕРБУРГЬ, 1876). For a brief description of the exhibits of the Russian technical schools see: "Exhibits of Foreign Technical Schools at the Centennial," *Scientific American*, Vol. 35, no. 8, August 19, 1876, p. 120.
27 "The Russian System of Trade Education," *Scientific American*, Vol. 35, no. 17, October 21, 1876, p. 265. For a description of Della Vos and his methods see: Charles A. Bennet, *History of Manual and Industrial Education, 1870-1917* (Peoria, IL: Industrial Arts Press, 1937), chapter I.
28 Victor Della Vos, *Description of the Collections of Scientific Appliances Instituted for the Study of Mechanical Art in Workshops of the Imperial Technical School of Moscow* (Moscow, 1876), p. xix.
29 Bennett, op. cit., pp. 17-18.
30 "Exhibits of Foreign Technical Schools at the Centennial," *Scientific American*, Vol. 35, no. 8, August 19, 1876, p. 120.
31 Quoted by Bennett, op. cit., p. 320.
32 Della Vos, op. cit., p. xiv.
33 Bennett, op. cit., p. 322.
34 John Runkle, "The Manual Element in Education," *Forty First Annual Report of the Board of Education, State of Massachusetts, 1876-77*, reprinted by Bennett, op. cit., p. 342.
35 Ibid.
36 John Runkle, "The Russian System of Mechanical Art Education, as Applied in the Massachusetts institute of Technology," *National Education Association of the*

United States. *Addresses and Proceedings* (Louisville, KY, 1877), p. 327. This quote by Buchanan is included in a series of general remarks at the end of Runkle's article.
37. *Ibid.*, p. 238.
38. Lawrence Cremin, *The Transformation of the School* (New York: Alfred A. Knopf, 1961), p. 28. For a detailed biography of Woodward see: Charles m. Dye, "Calvin Woodward and Manual Training: The Man, the Idea and the School," *The Bulletin* (Missouri Historical Society), Vol. 32, no. 3, January 1976, pp. 75-98.
39. Cremin, *op. cit.*, p. 26 and Dye, *op. cit.*, p. 76.
40. *Ibid.*, p. 82. C. M. Woodward, *The Manual Training School* (Boston: D. C. Heath & Co., 1887), pp. 277-280.
41. Quoted by I. Edwards Clarke, *Industrial and High Art Education in the United States, Part I. Drawing in the Public Schools* (Washington, DC: Government Printing Office, 1885).
42. *Ibid.*, p. 49.
43. Harris, *op. cit.*, p. 191.
44. *Ibid.*, p. 192.
45. For a detailed history of the early development of art education in the Massachusetts schools see: Clarke, *op. cit.*, pp. 37-61.
46. Newspaper clipping from the *Chicago Tribune*, June 1, 1876, included in Volume 4 of the *Centennial Scrapbooks*, City Archives of Philadelphia. For a complete description of the materials included in the Massachusetts art exhibit see: *Department of Education and Science: Catalogue of Some of the Prominent Exhibits in This Department from Massachusetts* (Philadelphia: A. C. Bryson & Co., 1876).
47. Hodgins, *op. cit.*, pp. 115-116.
48. *Ibid.*, pp. 106, 111, 113, 115, 207, 222 and 243.
49. See for example the editorial article in *The Atlantic Monthly*, October 1876, entitled "Characteristics of the International Fair," which includes a detailed description of the various drawing exhibits, pp. 492-493.
50. Harris, *op. cit.*, p. 203.
51. Harris, *op. cit.*, pp. 168-171.
52. Nearly the entire St. Louis School exhibit has been preserved as part of the educational collection of the St. Louis Public Library. In addition to volumes of examination papers and drawings done by students is a portfolio of over one hundred photographs of schools in and around St. Louis. Among the most interesting of these photographs are pictures of the Des Peres Kindergarten, which is commonly recognized as the first successful public kindergarten in the United States. A complete catalogue of the St. Louis school exhibit is included in Harris, "The Centennial Exhibition," *op. cit.*, pp. 168-171.
53. Hodgins, *op. cit.*, p. 15.

54 *Pennsylvania at the Centennial Exhibition of 1876* (Harrisburg, PA: B. F. Meyers, 1875), p. 5.
55 Harrington, *op. cit.*, p. 268.
56 For background on the history of the kindergarten in the United States see: Nina C. Vandelwalker, *The Kindergarten in American Education* (New York: The MacMillan Co., 1908); International Kindergarten Union Committee of Nineteen, *Pioneers of the Kindergarten in America* (New York: Teachers College Press, 1969); Agnes Snyder, *Dauntless Women in Childhood Education, 1856-1931* (Washington, DC: Association for Childhood Education International, 1972); and Elizabeth D. Ross, *The Kindergarten Crusade* (Athens: Ohio University Press, 1976).
57 Weber, *op. cit.*, pp. 30-33. While Boston has the honor of having had the first publicly supported kindergarten, which was set up under the direction of Elizabeth Peabody in 1869, the experiment failed and was discontinued.
58 *Ibid.* Concerning the need to demonstrate the kindergarten process rather than the kindergarten materials, Elizabeth Peabody argued that: "To show, therefore the materials of play, is not enough; without showing how they are used;..." See: Elizabeth Peabody, "Centennial Kindergarten in the Annex of the Women's Pavilion," *Kindergarten Messenger (New England Journal of Education)*, 4, December 16, 1876, p. 273.
59 Elizabeth Peabody, "Centennial Kindergarten," *Kindergarten Messenger (New England Journal of Education)*, 3, no. 6, June 1875, p. 121.
60 *Ibid.*
61 Bertha A. Winkler, "Ruth R. Burritt," *Women's Word's*, 4, no. 9, January, 1881, p. 607.
62 *Ibid.*
63 Peabody, "Centennial Kindergarten in the Annex to the Women's Pavilion," p. 273.
64 *Ibid.*
65 Frank Lloyd Wright, *An Autobiography* (New York: Duell, Sloan and Pearce, 1943), p. 13.
66 *Ibid.*, p. 14.
67 See for example Grant Carpenter Manson, *Frank Lloyd Wright to 1910* (New York: Reinhold Publishing Corporation, 1958), pp. 5-10.
68 Nina C. Vandelwalker in her earlier cited history of kindergarter education in the United States wrote concerning the demonstration kindergarten that: "Thousands thronged to see the new educational departure, and many remained hours afterwards to ask questions. The Exposition marked an epoch in the advancement of the kindergarten movement..." *The Kindergarten in American Education*, pp. 18-19.

69 International Exhibition, Department of Education and Science, *Catalogue of Some of the Prominent Exhibits in this Department From Massachusetts* (Philadelphia: A. C. Bryson & Co., 1876), p. 3.
70 Elizabeth Peabody, *Kindergarten Messenger* (*New England Journal of Education*), 6, June 10, 1876, p. 285.
71 Hodgins, *op. cit.*, pp. 54–57. Considerable interest was shown by foreigners in the Pennsylvania educational exhibit. As James P. Wickersham explained in his work, *A History of Education in Pennsylvania, Private and Public, Elementary and Higher* (Lancaster, PA.: Published for the author), as quoted from the *School Journal*:

> Besides, the Hall is the constant resort of foreigners seeking information on the subject of American education. Gentlemen connected with almost every nation represented at the exposition have visited it for this purpose—among them Russians, Austrians, Hungarians, Germans, Italians, Frenchmen, Swedes, Norwegians, Japanese, Chinese, Belgians, Hollanders, Swiss, Canadians, and South Americans of various nationalities. The Emperor of Brazil, Dom Pedro, made an early morning visit to the Hall, uninvited, and with a view to special study, accompanied by a single attendant, and spent some two hours alone in examining what is to be seen. He expressed himself very pleased with the exhibit, and took occasion subsequently to show that such was that fact. And, be it understood, the visits of these foreigners are not the visits of mere sight-seers, but are made mostly by persons in official position, or such as to come to the Exposition charged with the duty of investigating educational systems. (p. 580).

72 As early as 1874, the American Commissioner of Education proposed that an international conference be held in conjunction with the Centennial Exposition. Plans for the conference were never completed and the "informal" conference was held instead.
73 Department of the Interior, Bureau of Education, *The International Conference on Education Held at Philadelphia July 17 and 18 in Conjunction with the International Exhibition of 1876* (Washington, DC: Government Printing Office, 1877), pp. 3–4.
74 *Ibid.*, p. 12.
75 United States Bureau of Education. *Public Libraries in the United States of America: Their History, Condition and Management.* Special Report, Part I (Washington, DC: United States Government Printing Office, 1876).
76 *Ibid.*, pp. 623–648.
77 For an analysis of Dewey and the library movement in general see: Dee Garrison, *Apostles of Culture* (New York: The Free Press, 1979).
78 Melvil Dewey, "Decimal Classification Beginnings," *Library Journal*, February 15, 1920, p. 152.
79 *Ibid.*

80 United States Bureau of Education, *Public Libraries in the United States of America*, op. cit., p. 624.
81 *The Chronicles of '74 Since Graduation from Amherst College* (Warren, Mass.: 1885), p. 16. Quoted by Fremont Rider, *Melvil Dewey* (Chicago: American Library Association, 1944), pp. 20-21.
82 Northrup, op. cit., p. 28.
83 Birdsey Grant Northrup, *Lessons from European Schools and the American Centennial* (New York: A. S. Barnes & Co., 1877), p. 64.
84 Ibid., p. 83.
85 Quoted by Hodgins, op. cit., p. 97.
86 A. Tolman Smith, "The Indian Education Exhibit," *New England Journal of Education*, 4, no. 10, p. 15.
87 Hodgins, op. cit., p. 75.
88 Ibid.
89 Ibid., pp. 285-287.
90 Northrup, *Lessons from European Schools and the American Centennial*, p. 73.
91 Ibid.
92 "Congressional Proceedings, Forty-Fourth Congress, 1875-1877," included in William Jones Rhees, ed., *The Smithsonian Institution, Documents related to its Origins and History. 1835-1894*, Vol. I (Washington, DC: Government Printing Office, 1901), p. 749.
93 Ibid., p. 750.
94 Ibid., p. 757.
95 Ibid., p. 751.
96 Ibid., p. 743.
97 Ibid., p. 769. For background on the "Castle" and the "Arts and Industry Building" see: James M. Goode, "The Arts and Industries Building," included in Robert C. Post, ed., *1876: A Centennial Exhibition* (Washington, DC: The National Museum of History and Technology, 1976), pp. 209-213.
98 Ibid., p. 761.
99 Circular letter, John Eaton to school superintendent, city and state boards of education, etc., Washington, D.C., March 24, 1875. Attached to this letter is the "Synopsis of the proposed Centennial History of American Education—1776-1876," included in the general collection, Sterling Library, Yale University.
100 "Education at the International Exhibition," *Report of the Commissioner of Education for the Year 1875* (Washington, DC: Government Printing Office, 1875), pp. cxliv-cxlv.
101 Ibid.

102 Lawrence A. Cremin, *The Wonderful World of Ellwood Patterson Cubberley: An Essay of the Historiography of American Education* (New York: Teachers College, Columbia University, 1965), p. 12.

103 Among the educational histories that were specially prepared for the Centennial exhibition were: John Swett, *History of the Public School System of California* (San Francisco: A. L. Bancroft and Co., 1876); James H. Smart, *The Indiana Schools and the Men Who Have Worked in Them* (Cincinnatti, OH: Wilson, Hinkle and Co., 1876?); W. C. Whitfrod, *Historical Sketch of Education in Wisconsin* (Madison, WI: Atwood and Culver, 1876); and Thomas B. Stockwell, ed., *A History of Public Education in Rhode Island from 1636 to 1876* (Providence: Providence Press Co., 1876).

104 Ellwood P. Cubberley, *Public Education in the United States: A Study and Interpretation of American Educational History* (Boston: Houghton Mifflin Company, 1934, first edition, 1919).

105 Cremin, *The Wonderful World of Ellwood Patterson Cubberley*, op. cit.

106 Cubberley, op. cit., p. viii.

107 Ibid., p. ix.

108 Cremin, *The Wonderful World of Ellwood Patterson Cubberley*, op. cit., p. 47.

109 Bernard Bailyn, *Education in the Forming of American Society* (New York: W. W. Norton, 1960), p. 9.

110 "Education at the International Exhibition," *Report of the Commissioner of Education for the Year 1875*, op. cit., pp. cxliv-cxlv.

111 Cubberley, op. cit., p. 762.

112 E. E. White, "Technical Training in American Schools," *Circular of Information of the Bureau of Education*, no. 3-1881 (Washington, DC: Government Printing Office, 1881), p. 22.

113 Ibid.

Chapter 3
The World's Columbian Exposition

The Ferris Wheel at the World's Columbian Exhibition, symbol of the Fair. Courtesy of the Library of Congress.

The Chicago 1893 World's Columbian Exposition marked the end of an era. "The White City," as the Exposition came to be known, was created in a town that had been incorporated only a few years before the Civil War and whose growth and development served as a measure of the United States' rapid expansion and growth during the second half of the nineteenth century.

Considering Chicago's relatively brief history as a city, and its location on the edge of the frontier, it was particularly appropriate that at the meeting of the American Historical Association held at the World's Columbian Exposition, the American historian Frederick Jackson Turner delivered his classic paper "The Significance of the Frontier in American History."

Turner summarized an argument that had been popular since the 1830s: "...the existence of an area of free land, its continuous recession, and the advance of the American settlement westward, explain American development."[1]

Turner's "Frontier Thesis" became the most important interpretation of American history to emerge from the late nineteenth century. According to him, as civilization was brought to the frontier, a process of social and political transformation took place that saw the aristocratic republican democracy of Thomas Jefferson transformed into the broader democracy of Andrew Jackson and Abraham Lincoln: "In the crucible of the frontier the immigrants were Americanized, liberated and fused into a mixed race." Chicago, the city that hosted the World's Columbian Exposition, could be pointed to as a demonstration of this argument.

The coming together of diverse cultures and people on the frontier, as part of the creation of a new American society, was seen by many as an inevitable result of social and cultural progress, and the Exposition itself was a visible manifestation of the United States' social, cultural and economic development.

It is not surprising, therefore, that as was the case with the Philadelphia Centennial Exhibition, the equation of knowledge and power—knowledge and progress—was repeated time and again by the organizers and observers of the exposition in Chicago.

One of the first problems that faced the sponsors of the Chicago exposition was how they should organize and classify the exhibits. As was the case in Philadelphia in 1876, as well as many subsequent expositions, the Smithsonian Institution contributed significantly to the conceptualization and organization of the fair.[2] Foremost among the staff from the Smithsonian Institution who worked on the development of the exposition in Chicago was G. Brown Goode.

Goode was the assistant secretary of the Smithsonian Institution and one of the leading figures in museum circles in the United States during the late nineteenth century. In Philadelphia in 1876, Goode had worked as an assistant curator under Spencer Fullerton Baird, naturalist and assistant secretary of the Smithsonian in charge of the National Museum. At the Centennial Exposition, Goode was responsible for planning and supervising the assembly of exhibits illustrating the animal and fishery resources of the United States. By 1879 he had become the head of the National Museum.[3]

Goode was first and foremost a museum curator and administrator. While he felt that the expositions possessed a great deal of educational value, he also was acutely aware of their specialized function. As he explained:

> The exposition or exhibition and fair are primarily for the promotion of industry and commerce; the museum for the advancement of learning.... The educational results of the expositions, though undeniably important, are chiefly incidental, and not at all proportionate to the prodigal expenditure of energy and money which are inseparable from every great exhibition.[4]

Palace of Mechanic Arts and lagoon at the World's Columbian Exposition, Chicago, Illinois, Frances Benjamin Johnston, photographer. Courtesy of the Library of Congress.

Yet despite these criticisms, Goode made a number of important contributions to the success of the World's Columbian Exposition. In his "First Draft of a System of Classification for the World's Columbian Exposition," he developed a basic rationale for the organization and selection of materials for the fair. For him, international expositions rather than being static were evolving or developing institutions. As he explained:

> The exhibition of the future will be an exhibition of ideas rather than of objects, and nothing will be deemed worthy of admission to its halls which has not some living, inspiring thought behind it, and which is not capable of teaching some valuable lesson.[5]

Goode understood the purpose of the exposition in Chicago to be to provide a history of the American continent since the arrival of the first European settlers, and to demonstrate the influence of the United States on the history of the world. The exposition would according to him:

> ...expound, as far as may be, the steps of progress of civilization and its arts in successive centuries, and in all lands up to the present time and their present condition; to be in fact, *an illustrated encyclopedia of civilization*.[6]

Like others involved in the expositions, Goode saw progress as being the principal or guiding theme of the world's fairs.

To some extent, it can be argued that the expositions represented for the people who organized and visited them a dynamic interpretation of the new industrial culture that was emerging around them. As Robert Rydell has explained, the international expositions provided "millions of fairgoers in the wake of industrial depressions and outbursts of class warfare" a "cohesive explanatory blueprint of social experience."[7]

Rydell's interpretation is substantiated by visitors to Chicago. Henry Adams—perhaps the most astute observer and social commentator to visit the World's Columbian Exposition—asked in response to its massive displays, machinery and elaborate architectural facades "whether the American people knew where they were driving."[8] Jostled by the confusion of the Exposition and its meaning, Adams recalled how:

> ...one turned to the exhibits for help and found it. The industrial schools tried to teach so much and so quickly that the instruction ran to waste. Some millions of other people felt the same helplessness, but few of them were seeking education, and to them helplessness seemed natural and normal, for

they had grown up in the habit of thinking a steam engine or a dynamo as natural as the sun,...⁹

For Adams, the exposition in Chicago represented a carefully defined symbolic system—one which confirmed many Americans' belief in the icons of knowledge and power. The Exposition forced individuals to recognize the new material and symbolic universe into which they had entered:

> Education ran riot at Chicago, at least for retarded minds which had never faced in concrete form so many matters of which they were ignorant. Men who knew nothing whatever—who had never run a steam-engine, the simplest of forces—who had never put their hands on a lever—had never touched an electric battery—never talked through a telephone, and had not the shadow of a notion what amount of force was meant by a *watt* or an *ampere* or an *erg*, or any other term of measurement introduced within a hundred years—had no choice but to sit down on the steps and brood as they had never brooded on the benches of Harvard College, either as student or professor...¹⁰

It was hoped by the organizers of the Fair that the lessons learned at the World's Columbian Exposition would be communicated to future generations, not just to those visiting the Fair. As Potter Palmer, president of the World's Columbia Commission explained at the dedication of the exposition on October 12, 1892:

> May we not hope that lessons here learned, transmitted to the future, will be potent forces long after the multitudes which will throng these aisles shall have measured their span and faded away.¹¹

Palmer's hopes were in fact realized by Francis J. Bellamy, one of the editors of the children's magazine the *Youth's Companion*, when he devised a plan that would make the children across the nation part of the great celebration of Columbus's discovery of America. Bellamy urged that the dedication day of the Fair, October 12, 1892, be set aside as a national holiday. Children would come together in schools and churches across the country to celebrate Columbus's discovery and the exposition being held in Chicago to commemorate it. In order to make the event truly national in character Bellamy drafted the "Pledge of Allegiance to the Flag of the United States." Copies of the pledge were circulated to teachers throughout the country by the United States Department of Education. The directors of the Exposition, as well as presidential candidates Harrison and Cleveland endorsed Bellamy's project.¹²

Pledge of Allegiance in a Washington, D.C. school, 1899, Frances Benjamin Johnston, photographer. Courtesy of the Library of Congress.

By means of the Pledge of Allegiance, countless students were drawn together in their celebration of the nation and its four-hundred-year history. As Annie Randell White, author of a children's history of Columbus and the Fair, reminded her readers, the exposition in Chicago "involved more than an exhibit of wonderful productions. It means a new era in the onward march of civilization."[13]

The World's Columbian Exposition opened in May of 1893. According to Robert Rydell, it

> ...served as an exercise in educating the nation on the concept of progress as a *willed* national activity toward a determined, utopian goal.[14]

Education and the power imparted by new forms of knowledge would provide the means by which this utopian ideal would be achieved.

The education exhibits at the World's Columbian Exposition were as extensive as any held up until that time. Thirty-two states sent major exhibits to the Exposition, while a total of forty-four states were in some way represented.[15] Twenty-six foreign countries contributed to the educational exhibits, the principal contributions coming from Germany, France, England, Canada, New South Wales, Russia, Mexico, Brazil and Japan. Over two-thirds of the exhibits were displayed on the second floor of the Manufactures and Liberal Arts Building, while the rest of the exhibits were scattered in buildings throughout the Exposition. The space devoted to the exhibits was enormous—259,600 square feet being assigned in the Liberal Arts Building alone, and approximately 100,000 square feet of display space elsewhere.

World's Columbian Exposition: Liberal Arts Building, Chicago, United States, 1893. Liberal Arts Building, Grand Basin and North Canal, [with gondolas on canal and people in view,] Sept.; Starks W. Lewis, Amateur, Brooklyn, N.Y. Brooklyn Museum Archives, Goodyear Archival Collection.

Writing about the educational exhibits at Chicago, John Eaton, the former United States Commissioner of Education, once again repeated the equation of knowledge and power that had so dominated the rhetoric of the Philadelphia Centennial Exposition. In observing visitors to the Exposition he explained how, one

> ...can neither mingle in the throng nor look upon it without being filled with meditations upon the deepest educational problems and the effects of their solution upon man's destiny.[16]

According to him, the object learning provided for the masses visiting the Exposition was without parallel:

> Have we ever given up our souls to the influence of the mighty forces of nature—the boundless forest, the measureless prairie, the torrent of Niagara, or the fathomless ocean? Here in this presence not only a material mass lays upon us resistless, unutterable power, but we feel that there is in it a spirit with a destiny above it—a spirit to abide when all else that is visible disappears to triumph over the wreck of worlds, godlike in its possibilities and godward in its aspirations, which it is our duty to promote. For this purpose we are teachers.[17]

Crowds of people at the opening day of the World's Columbian Exposition. Courtesy of the Library of Congress.

Eaton is describing what is perhaps the most characteristic of all American myths: that we as Americans are somehow a chosen people, a people who by divine right are destined to lead the lesser nations of the earth to enlightened civilization and government.

This myth is one that dates back to the beginning of the Colonial era, when John Winthrop told the group of Puritans he was leading to the New World that:

> We shall find the God of Israel is among us, when ten of us shall be able to resist a thousand of our enemies, when he shall make us a praise and a glory, that men shall say of succeeding plantations [settlements]: the Lord make it like that of New England: for we must Consider that we shall be as a City upon a Hill, the eyes of all people are upon us.[18]

Grand Finale of the Stupendous Spectacular Success, "Uncle Sam's Show." *Puck.* **Courtesy of the Library of Congress.**

Implicit in this vision of America as being a "City upon a Hill" is not only the assumption of the United States being a nation favored by God, but that the values of its people are superior to those of other nations.

According to Eaton, education—and the direction found within American democracy—provided an antidote to the disorder and disruption that most nations were faced with:

Taking the exhibit of education in connection with other portions of the Exposition, one cannot fail to be impressed with the power of education in saving nations from disorder, and imparting to them conditions of national progress.[19]

Education would provide the means by which to draw together the nations of the world into a single unified order. Through education mankind would be able to achieve "mastery over nature," and continue "his triumphant progress in the destiny divinely offered him."[20]

Eaton's belief that the Chicago Exposition was part of a larger movement involving the unification of the nations of the world into a single rational system was repeated by others commenting on the Fair. The American philosopher and educator Denton J. Snider wrote, for example, that:

> The nations are going toward a common civilization, nay toward a common government. The Asiatic confusion of the Plaisance is moving—has to move—into the universal order, which is hinted in the Exposition.[21]

According to Snider, the examples set by the "civilized world," in particular the United States would lead the nations of the world to a higher level of civilization and culture.

The fact that the model set by the "civilized world" was racist and reflected the social, political and cultural domination of a selected business and industrial class tended to be overlooked. This argument has been clealry demonstrated by Robert Rydell in his study *All the World's A Fair*. According to him the ethnological exhibits assembled for the various international expositions provided the "intellectual scaffolding" for a "cumulative symbolic universe." As he explains:

> This symbolic construct centered on the interpretation of Darwinian theories about racial development and utopian dreams about America's material and national progress. Central to the presentation of this constellation of ideas as a valid interpretation of social reality were ethnological exhibits furnished by both reputable anthropologists and well-financed showmen. Anthropological attractions—consisting of cultural artifacts, lay-figure groupings of "primitive types," and selected nonwhites living in ethnological villages along the midways—charted a course of racial progress toward an image of utopia that was reflected in the main exposition buildings.[22]

The ethnological exhibits, according to Rydell, were largely limited to the exposition midways. At the 1876 Philadelphia Centennial Exposition these midways were relegated to locations outside of the official exhibit grounds and were not officially sanctioned. Although located at the edge of the exhibit grounds, the Midway Plaisance at the World's Columbian Exposition was officially classified under the fair's Department of Ethnology.[23] By 1904 the organizers of the Louisiana Purchase Exposition in St. Louis had incorporated the midway or "Pike" into the main exposition grounds.[24]

At Chicago, Frederick Ward Putnam, the head of Harvard's Peabody Museum of American Archaeology and Ethnology, was hired to direct the exposition's anthropological exhibits. Separate exhibits were also mounted by the Smithsonian, as well as a number of foreign exhibitors. The main inspiration for the ethnological exhibits at Chicago was the tenth Congress Internationale d'Anthropologie et d' Archeologie Prehistoriques that was held as part of the 1889 Paris Exposition,[25] where a colonial city was set up that included 182 Asians and Africans living in simulated native villages.[26]

Samuel Pierpont Langley together with G. Brown Goode drew heavily on the Paris exhibits as a model when they first proposed the Smithsonian's ethnological displays at Chicago. Their purpose would be:

> ...to show the physical and other characteristics of the principal races of men and the very early stages of the history of civilization as shown by the evolution of certain selected primitive arts and industries.[27]

Display of Indian culture and life by the Smithsonian Institution and National Museum. Courtesy of the Smithsonian Institution.

Such an approach would conform with Goode's intention to classify the exhibits at the exposition so as to demonstrate the progress of civilization.[28]

Putnam hoped that the ethnological exhibit at Chicago would lead to the establishment of a major museum at Chicago.[29] In fact, his hopes were realized when Marshall Field and other Chicago business leaders decided to institutionalize selected exhibits from the exposition in a permanent museum. Chicago's Field Museum was established as a result—one of the more interesting and important educational outcomes of the fair.[30]

Ethnographic exhibits were included in a specially constructed Anthropology Building, as well as in the Government Building. It was the "living" exhibits on the Midway Plaisance, however, that were to attract the greatest attention. The living ethnology exhibits led to some interesting—and disturbing juxtapositions. Talking about the Irish and Egyptian exhibits on the midway, John Eaton commented, for example, that:

> Here in the Irish Village and In Donegal Castle we may examine the much-needed application of instruction to the improvement of Irish industries. In the school in the Streets of Cairo the pupils are seated on the floor, after the oriental fashion, and studying aloud. If we choose, before leaving the Midway, we may compare the influence of training upon wild animals, such as the lion and ostrich.[31]

The inclusion of the ethnography exhibits on the midway—including "living classrooms"—was repeated at subsequent expositions such as the 1904 Louisiana Purchase Exposition in St. Louis. Their organization and presentation confirmed the tendency of the organizers of the Fair to assume the superiority of American and European models of culture and learning. According to Rydell:

> Hailed as a "great object lesson" in anthropology by leading anthropologists, the Midway provided visitors with ethnological, scientific sanction for the American view of the nonwhite world as barbaric and childlike and gave a scientific basis to the racial blueprint for building a utopia.... On the Midway at the World's Columbian Exposition, evolution, ethnology, and other popular amusements interlocked as active agents and bulwarks of hegemonic assertion of ruling-class authority. [32]

Of all the groups that attracted attention as part of the ethnographic exhibits, the North American Indian exhibits were almost certainly the most popular. The North American Indian exhibits were located in a number of different locations. On the Midway Plaisance was a cement and stucco reconstruction of Colorado's Battle Mountain. Called the Cliff Dweller's exhibit, this five story structure contained extensive collections of Southwest Indian artifacts, including models of Anasazi ruins in Mancos.[33] In the Anthropological Building were static exhibits, developed by Putnam for the Smithsonian, that focused on comparing Native Americans with other "primitive" cultures from around the world.[34] The Commissioner of Indian Affairs Thomas Morgan was also involved in bringing Native American exhibits to the Fair. Adjacent to, and technically part of, Putnam's Anthropology Building was a two-story frame schoolhouse. During the fair, groups of students from government schools were housed in the building. Attracting over one hundred thousand visitors a week during the summer, the Indian exhibit demonstrated, according to Commissioner Morgan, the Indian's "readiness and ability for the new conditions of civilized life and American citizenship upon which he is entering."[35]

Egyptian dancing girl, World's Columbian Exhibition, Chicago, Illinois. Courtesy of the Library of Congress.

Frederick Hoxie in his work *A Final Promise: The Campaign to Assimilate the Indians, 1880–1920* argues that the separation of the Bureau of Indian Affairs exhibit under Commissioner Morgan and Putnam's exhibits in the Anthropological Building was more than a "bureaucratic convenience."

> ...the two exhibits were strikingly different. One conveyed the idea that the Indians were members of an exotic race with little connection to modern

America. The other, by stressing education and native "progress," pointed to the possibility of Indian assimilation.[36]

Captain Richard Henry Pratt, Headmaster of the Carlisle School, was furious about Putnam's representation of Indian life and culture. He was convinced that Putnam's efforts acted as reminders of the Indian's "barbaric" past. In viewing the exhibits, the public would be distracted from the important progress Indian groups had achieved.[37]

Pratt wanted nothing to do with Putnam's exhibits at Chicago. Obtaining space for a Carlisle room in the Liberal Arts Building, he also received permission to have his students march in the fair's opening-day parade.[38] Carrying a banner inscribed "Into Civilization and Citizenship," Pratt recalled in his autobiography how:

> ...the students were divided into ten platoons, each representing a characteristic of the school, through which we expected them to attain civilization qualities and citizenship. The first platoon carried school books and slates. The second represented printing; the front rank students carried sticks, galleys, cases, etc., and the rear rank papers and pamphlets which they had printed. The third represented agriculture, the front rank carrying agricultural implements, the rear rank the products of agriculture from our school farms. The fourth platoon represented our baking department, the front carrying paddles, ovenpeels, etc., the rear rank bread. The fifth represented carpentry, the front bearing tools, the rear specimens of their skill in woodwork. The sixth represented blacksmithing, the front rank bearing tools, the rear rank horseshoes, chains, etc. The seventh represented shoemaking, the front rank carrying knives, lasts, hammers, etc., the rear rank shoes. The eighth represented harness making, the front rank bearing tools, the rear rank parts of the harness, etc. The ninth represented tinsmithing, the front rank carrying shears, mallets and other tools, the rear rank buckets, coffee pots, etc. The tenth and last platoon represented tailoring, the front rank carrying lapboards, shears, tailor's goose, etc., the rear rank madeup clothing.[39]

Pratt described the need to establish the Carlisle exhibit as growing directly out of the "opposite and inimical purposes" of both the Indian and Ethnological Bureaus. According to him in contradistinction to these two exhibits:

> Carlisle's exhibit showed how the Indian could learn to march in line with America as a very part of it, heads up, eyes front, where he could see his glorious future of manly competition in citizenship and be on an equality as an individual.[40]

Pratt felt that the Smithsonian exhibits and those of the government's Indian Bureau were:

> ...calculated to keep the nation's attention and the Indian's energies fixed upon his valueless past, through the spectacular aboriginal housing, dressing and curio implements it instituted. The illustrative boarding school in their exposition camps said to the Indians: "You may have some of our education, but not enough to enable you to become one of us. You are to remain a separate and peculiar people, and continue under our Bureau supervision."[41]

Pratt's opposition to the Bureau of Indian Affair's exhibit made him *persona non grata* with Thomas J. Morgan—the bureau's commissioner. Offered by Morgan to take charge of the Bureau's boarding school exhibit in the Fall of 1891, Pratt refused, objecting to the "noted ethnologist living in Washington" (Putnam) who was going to be responsible for organizing the larger Indian exhibit.[42]

Others objected to the exhibits organized by Putnam and Morgan as well. Emma Sickles, who was employed for a short time as a member of Putnam's staff and then fired, was quoted by the *New York Times* as saying that "the World's Fair is being used to further one of the darkest conspiracies ever conceived against the Indian race."[43] According to Sickles, Putnam and Morgan created:

> An exhibit of savagery in its most repulsive form, participated in by only the lowest specimens of the Indian race or by those noted for bloodthirsty deeds. These savages show the need of Government officials to civilize them, and furnish argument to those who wish to drive them from their homes or plot to handle their money.[44]

Significantly, the models presented by Putnam and Morgan, versus those of Pratt and Sickles, both represented assimilation of the Native American populations. Putnam and Morgan's models, however, seem in retrospect linked much more closely to models based on domination and hegemony involving the inevitable triumph of white mainstream culture and civilization over the Indian population. A newspaper correspondent summed up the situation clearly when he described how several Sioux chiefs appeared at the closing of the fair's opening ceremonies just as the chorus began singing "My Country 'Tis of Thee." Describing the effect of the scene, he explained that:

> Nothing in the day's occurrences appealed to sympathetic patriotism so much as this fallen majesty slowly filing out of sight as the flags of all nations swept

satin kisses through the air, waving congratulations to cultured achievement and submissive admiration to a new world.[45]

The self-confidence elicited by most Americans at the Chicago Exposition about the superiority of their culture was challenged by many foreign educators visiting the Exposition. Professor Stephen Waetzoldt, who was a member of the educational delegation from Germany commented in a lecture in Berlin shortly after the Exposition that:

> Americans consider themselves more intelligent than all other nations. An American never thinks slightingly of himself; he believes himself to be the man of the future, conscious that nothing within the limits of human power and ingenuity is impossible for him.[46]

According to Waetzoldt, by comparison with Germany and other European countries, the United States appeared to be a country where class distinctions were nowhere near as rigid. Education was therefore seen by him as playing a much more crucial role in the definition of class and social status than in Europe. Another German visitor to the Exposition Professor Emil Hausknecht observed:

> In America—at least as yet—everyone, even a common laborer, may become anything and everything, even President if he understands how and has learned enough to make wise use of circumstances. It is quite immaterial how he acquired his knowledge, or whether he can by written testimonials prove to be in possession of such knowledge.[47]

According to Hausknecht, the intense desire of the laboring classes in the United States to receive a practical education was a logical result of the fact that education was perceived as providing the key to social advancement in the United States.

Other foreign visitors left detailed impressions of the Exposition and the American educational system. The Frenchman Jules Violle, for example, observed how:

> The Exposition at Chicago has shown with what vigor all branches of human activity are developed in the United States. Certainly science has not yet attained heights comparable with those on which at present the fortune of capitalists is elevated; the dollar holds first place, but science advances with rapid steps.... The Americans comprehend that high intellectual culture is not alone a question of elegant luxuriance or national self-love; the prosperity and even the future of the country depends upon it.[48]

Economic and industrial development were seen as being inextricably linked to education and that the country's very future was dependent upon the development of education.

In conjunction with the Chicago Exposition, a series of World Congresses were held. Their purpose according to their chairman was:

> ...to provide for the proper presentation of the intellectual and moral progress of the world by a series of international conferences of the leaders in all the chief departments of human achievements.[49]

The most prominent and widely-publicized of these congresses was the Religious Congress or "Parliament of Religions" that was held in early September. Of nearly equal interest and importance was the International Congress on Education. Fifteen departments were represented in the Congress: Higher Education, Secondary, Elementary, School Supervision, the Professional Training of Teachers, Rational Psychology, Educational Publications, Business Publications, Kindergarten Education, Art, Vocal Music, Technological Instruction, Industrial and Manual Instruction, Physical Education and Experimental Psychology in Education.[50]

The Congress opened on the afternoon of July 25, 1893. Under the supervision of the National Education Association, the Congress was directed by William Torrey Harris, the United States Commissioner of Education. Representatives from nearly all of the major foreign exhibits were in attendance, as well as from many of the country's major school systems and universities.[51]

In his opening remarks to the Educational Congress William Torrey Harris once again reiterated the theme of knowledge and power—education and progress. According to Harris the renewed interest being taken in education by the various nations of the world was cause "for congratulation among all the friends of human progress."

For Harris, education represented one of the main movements responsible for the regeneration of modern society. According to him, education and the schools provided the individual with the main means available for self-help. As he remarked in his opening comments: "Education gives directive power—the power to combine things, and the power to combine men."[52]

The unifying force provided by education was a theme that was also discussed at great length by other speakers at the Educational Congress. James B. Angell, the president of the University of Michigan, at the opening of the Second General Session argued:

...that the work of these educational congresses underlies in some sense, the work of all the other congresses which have been or which may be held at this time. Perhaps I might better say that the work of this congress overarches, enfolds, and encompasses the work of all of the other congresses, as the sky encompasses and enfolds the earth; for all art, and all science—what hope of progress have these, what hope of perpetuity have they, except as the moral and intellectual discipline which we are engaged in cultivating is preserved.[53]

Throughout the introductory remarks made by the various speakers at the Educational Congress, the idea of education providing the means of elevating the culture or society of which it is a part is repeated over and over again. G. W. Ross, the Ontario Minister of Education, elaborated on this theme by emphasizing the education of the masses. According to him:

...the watchword of the nineteenth century is, Educate the masses!... Go, educate these people who are soon to control the destinies of the nation; and educate the teachers so that they shall rise to a higher plane...[54]

As M. Ergraff Kovalesky, delegate of the Russian Ministry of Public Instruction explained, the role of the pedagogue or educator was that of a tool which would raise the culture to a higher level of civilization. For him, America's educators represented "the spiritual builders of modern progress in the United States."[55]

Going beyond the rhetoric of many of the introductory speeches made at the Educational Congress, was the exchange of a great deal of substantive information about education. In many respects, the educational meetings held at Chicago functioned as a clearing house for the exchange of educational ideas on an international basis.[56] Going through the programs of the various meetings of the Educational Congresses, one cannot help but be impressed by not only the international representation, but by the pioneering efforts that were represented by the various invited guests and speakers.

In the Congress of Secondary Education, papers were presented concerning the education of women in France and England, and about appropriate methods of technical and scientific education. In the Congress of Physical Education papers were presented concerning innovative methods of physical training. Extensive presentations were made on issues dealing with social welfare and the need, for example, to provide playgrounds and parks for the poor. Figures such as G. Stanley Hall spoke on various aspects of the Child-Study Movement in America. David Star Jordan, the president of Stanford University and Charles Francis Adams argued for the elimination of Latin and Greek as a requirement for the bachelor's degree in American universities. Professor Woodrow Wilson of Princeton University presented a paper entitled "To what Extent Should an Antecedent Liberal Education be required of Students of Law, Medicine, and Theology?" Other educators making presentations at the Educational Congress included Seth Low of Columbia, Josiah Royce of Harvard University, Timothy Dwight of Yale University and James McCosh of Princeton University. Literally hundreds of presentations were made in the various educational congresses—presentations which represented on an international basis the most advanced pedagogical theories and philosophy of the period.

The sheer size and volume of the activities related to education at Chicago was overwhelming. Besides the Educational Congresses, there were of course the various exhibits that provided the main substance of the Exposition. In the case of the foreign exhibits, none was as extensive as that of Germany. Prepared under the direction of the German minister of education, and with the sanction of the Imperial Council, the German exhibit was housed primarily in the Manufacturers and Liberal Arts Building. Occupying approximately 16,000 square feet of exhibit space, the German educational exhibits were only superseded in size by the American educational exhibits.

While nearly all the states in the German Empire were represented in the educational display, it was Prussia who assumed the main responsibility for the cost and design of the exhibit. In doing so, a comprehensive display was assembled. Including all aspects of education from the university down to the rural elementary schools. Only the technical and gymnastic schools were excluded from the exhibit. A total of nearly 800 boxes measuring two cubic meters were eventually sent from Germany to make up the exhibit.

Upon entering the German exhibit, one encountered a display assembled by the Imperial Blind Assylum at Steiglitz. Included was an extensive Braille library. In addition, outlines were provided of methods for teaching blind students natural history, arithmetic, physics and geography, as well as models and pieces of constructive work put together by students in the assylum. Handiwork done by girls from the One Hundred and Forty Third Public School, statistics and photographs showing the growth of schools in Berlin, and examples of German pedagogical journals were included in the first section of the exhibit.

In a vestibule adjoining the main part of the German exhibit were displayed a series of photographs showing various aspects of scientific and gymnastic training. Included beneath these pictures were ten leather-bound portfolios containing architectural drawings of the Prussian schools. In the main display of the German exhibit were texts on the history of German education, statistical charts outlining the growth of school attendance and the decline of illiteracy in Germany, as well as school equipment. Rather than displaying only outstanding examples of student work, the German exhibit attempted to also show the work of typical students.

Critics of the German exhibit commented on the lack of textbooks in the display. In fact, textbooks were rarely used in the Prussian schools. Evidently most instruction was based on the individual knowledge of the instructor, which was communicated to the students as part of their normal lessons. Recognizing this fact as a fundamental difference between the German and American systems, Stephen Waetzoldt, professor at the University of Berlin, commented:

> Our tendency is to instruct totally as much as possible, and to make use of a book only when it is necessary for reference. The Americans teach by means of a textbook, not because of the inability of the teacher, but from pedagogical principles. Their idea is that in acquiring knowledge the pupil should not feel continually dependent upon the teacher, but himself do as much as possible.[57]

Visitors to the Columbian Exposition were able to observe an extraordinary array of demonstration classes. In his description of the educational exhibits at the exposition, John Eaton described a kindergarten in operation in the Illinois building and classes in Gymnastics at the Swedish exhibit.[58]

In the Children's Building—which was located adjacent to the Woman's Building—demonstration classes were mixed with a wide array of static exhibits. A model nursery, as well as instruction in Sloyd, a rooftop playground, a kindergarten, gymnastics classes under the sponsorship of the North American Turner Bund, and a class for deaf mutes were all on display.[59]

The Children's Building was financed by the Board of Lady Managers. Funds had been raised in large part by a bazaar at the home of Bertha Palmer, the president of the Board of Lady Managers.[60] Besides demonstration classes, activities conducted on a daily basis in the Children's Building included a series of lectures on nutrition and clothing for infants organized by Maria M. Love, as well as a supervised play house and day care facility. For twenty-five cents a day, parents could leave their child under the supervision of trained attendants. A total of 10,000 children were cared for by the service during the course of the Fair.[61]

Emerging technologies, such as the phonograph, made it possible for visitors to the educational exhibits to go beyond demonstration classes and actually "listen in" to the activities of classes from different parts of the country. Five different states including Iowa and Nebraska sent recordings on wax cylinders of classroom recitations, oral exams and music lessons.[62] Stephen Waetzoldt described how:

> ...seated in an easy chair, with the ends of the tubes of the Edison phonograph held to our ears and the large photograph of the class before us we heard the teachers instruct and the pupils answer. Thus we were enabled to pass judgement on a model lesson in history or grammar, and could convince ourselves of its correctness by the engrossed stenogram submitted.[63]

The educational exhibits and programs at the World's Columbian Exposition provided a unique opportunity for a wide-range of groups to place before the attention of both the nation and the world the work that they had done in the field of education. No one seized upon this opportunity more enthusiastically than the Catholic Church.

Plans for the educational exhibits in Chicago had from the very beginning included the participation of parochial schools. Catholic leaders saw the Exposition as providing an important opportunity to educate the country about the mission of the Catholic church and its schools. As the American educational historian James Sanders has explained in his book *The Education of an Urban Minority*:

> ...Catholics saw in the Columbian Exposition the opportunity to lay their schools open before the world. The psychology of a misunderstood minority trying to prove itself probably does more than anything else to explain the exaggerated efforts that went into the Chicago Catholic exhibit.[64]

On September 17, 1892 the Catholic newspaper the *New World* announced that the diocesan school board of Chicago had been empowered to prepare a plan of work and supervise the entire Catholic educational exhibit for the Exposition. A letter from the board in the September 24th issue of the *New World* asked the schools in the Chicago Diocese for their full cooperation in preparing the exhibits.[65] Exhibit materials were sent from across the country, as well as from Canada.

The Catholic Educational Exhibit was officially dedicated in July of 1893 by the Bishop of Peoria John Lancaster Spaulding. Located in the southeastern section of the Manufactures Building, the exhibit included 29,214 feet of floor space, 1,000 linear feet of aisles and 60,000 square feet of wall space. Nearly 1,200 exhibits were sent by different schools, religious teaching orders and dioceses from across the country, of which approximately one-fourth were actually used for the exhibit.

The Catholic Educational Exhibit at the World's Columbian Exhibition, Courtesy of the Library of Congress.

The Chicago Herald of June 5, 1893 wrote that the Catholic display was:

> ...an exhibit which should attract the attention and excite the admiration of all good people, be they Presbyterians, Methodists, Baptists, or the people who are responsible for the show. The Catholic Educational Exhibit is the feature referred to. It is not intended as a religious propaganda; it is simply a material exposition of what the people of one faith can do in the way of promoting humanity and the world's progress.[66]

The importance of the Fair in providing the Catholic community with an opportunity to present themselves in a favorable light to the nation was evident in the numerous congresses and meetings in which the Catholics participated. Chancellor of the Chicago Archdiocese, P. J. Muldoon explained that:

> The Catholic educational display has advanced among Catholics at one bold stroke the cause of Catholic education a quarter of a century, and among

non-Catholics it has undoubtedly dissipated prejudices that in the usual flow of events would not have been obliterated in fifty years.[67]

This desire for acceptance was repeated by other prominent Catholics who participated in activities in conjunction with the Fair. Archbishop Corrigan of New York, in a speech given as part of the Chicago Catholic Congress, argued that:

> Among those educated in our schools you will find no anarchists or socialists, but thousands and thousands of brave men and true, who love their country, not only for its own sake but for conscience' sake; who willingly obey its laws, and who would shed their blood in its defense.[68]

September 2, 1893 was designated as Catholic Education Day, and from September 4-9 a national Catholic Congress was held in conjunction with the Exposition. Descriptions of the educational displays indicate that they contained much of the same types of educational materials as displayed by the public schools from across the country.

Muldoon considered the Fair and the year 1893 as a turning point in the experience of American Catholics and their schools:

> The year 1893 will be the turning point in educational life. The difficulties of the past for Catholics have been many and severe. Thank God, as the country has prospered, we, one-sixth of its population, have shared in its prosperity, and our opportunities were never better, or our difficulties fewer than at present, and hence we may consistently hold fast to the safe-teaching "Catholic education for Catholic children."[69]

Implicit in his comments is the larger theme that dominated the international expositions in general—the theme of progress. Muldoon adopted the theme of knowledge and power, of knowledge and progress within a larger system of Catholic values and ethics. As he explained in his preface to *The World's Columbian Catholic Congress and Educational Exhibit*:

> Not knowledge only, not knowledge and morality merely, but religion, morality, and knowledge, sacred trinity of the powers of human progress, are essential to the proper education of the people.[70]

As was the case at the Philadelphia Centennial Exposition, the exhibits on manual and industrial training captured the interest of visitors to the Fair. If the Russian system of manual training dominated the attention of educators at the Philadelphia Centennial Exposition, then the Swedish sloyd method of industrial education was of particular interest to the educators who attended the World's Columbian Exposition in 1893. The term *sloyd* is difficult to translate literally into English. During the Middle Ages, the term was used to describe any type of trade or handiwork. In time, the meaning of the word came to be more restricted, until finally during the nineteenth century sloyd came to be associated with manual training where wood is employed as the primary material for instruction.[71]

The sloyd method has its origins in the rural folk and craft tradition of medieval Sweden. Forced by the bitter winters and the lack of sunlight in the Northern latitudes to stay inside, the Swedish peasantry turned to the manufacture of simple handmade objects. Men and boys would often carve simple tools for use in the home and on the farm. Women and young girls would spin, weave and knit. Families would work together, drawn around the hearth for warmth and companionship.[72]

The tradition of sloyd largely sustained itself until the end of the eighteenth century, at which time it was almost completely forgotten as part of the folkways of Swedish culture. Its decline can be attributed to a number of factors including an increase in the literacy rate of peasantry, the growth of industrialization with a consequential introduction of cheap manufactured household goods onto Swedish markets and finally a serious growth in the rate of alcoholism among the Swedish peasantry as a result of the legalization of the manufacture of home-made brandy. Yet despite the decline in the practice of sloyd, its tradition and the memory of a simpler and less complicated culture was never entirely forgotten. Beginning in the 1830s and 1840s the curriculums of many Swedish schools began to be loosely organized around sloyd activities. In 1846, a national association was established in order to promote sloyd and its adoption in the schools.[73]

By the 1870s numerous experiments had been made using sloyd in the schools. It was not until 1872, however, and the establishment of the Naas school near Gothenberg under the direction of Otto Salmon, that the sloyd method was carefully defined. Following many of the ideas of Uno Cygnaeus (1810-1888), an early Finnish teacher of sloyd, Salmon emphasized the following principles as being fundamental to the teaching of the method.[74]

1. Exercises done by the student should progress from the simple to the complex.
2. The exercises employed as part of the method should be as varied as possible—challenging the student while at the same time not overwhelming him.

3. The exercise should result in the making of a useful article from the very beginning. In doing so, the child will have a tangible object resulting from his labors of which he could be proud. Equally important, the child will be impressed with the fact that sloppy work will make a potentially valuable object worthless.
4. Any exercise done by the child should cultivate the child's aesthetic values by combining in the models beauty of form and proportion with utility.
5. Every model should be made in such a way that it can be drawn by students, rather than copied or traced.
6. Carving with a knife—an exercise that emphasizes manual dexterity and exactness with tools—should be the first thing the child is taught when he studies sloyd.[75]

Although having much the same purpose in mind, the differences between the Russian system and the sloyd system of manual training were enormous. The Russian system was based upon the principle of teaching the use of certain tools by making incomplete articles. The Russian system was devised primarily to develop skilled mechanics. Its purpose was strictly vocational. The sloyd method, on the other hand, was concerned with the special needs and particular capabilities of the growing child. Its purpose was to provide general education as well as specific vocational training.[76] In a presentation included as part of the International Congress of Education, Gustaf Larsson, the principal of the Sloyd Training School in Boston, Massachusetts, distinguished the difference between the Russian system and sloyd methods stating that:

> Sloyd methods are unlike Russian methods in giving great prominence to *form study*, and in the method by which all form work is made—methods which are quite unlike those of the carpenter, because the first care of the sloyd teacher is that the muscular sense of form be developed in the child rather than that the curves be accomplished in the quickest and easiest way.[77]

Articles describing the sloyd method had been published in the United States as early as 1882.[78] Yet the real influence of sloyd upon the American manual training movement did not begin until Gustaf Larson (1861-1919) came to Boston from Sweden in 1888. Looked upon by Otto Salomon as the Swedish representative of the sloyd movement in the United States, Larsson established the first successful American sloyd school shortly after his arrival in Boston.[79]

Larsson's first classes with children were held in a private school. In a few months, he was teaching a class demonstrating the sloyd method for a group of public school teachers. Eventually coming to the attention of the superintendent, Larsson was hired to work for the Boston public schools. Together with Frank M. Leavitt, who was familiar with the Russian system as a result of his training at the School of Mechanic Arts at the Massachusetts Institute of Technology, and Benjamin F. Eddy, a skilled craftsman trained in industry, Larsson established an experimental curriculum based on sloyd for the Boston schools. The experiment seems to have had as its purpose the eventual combination of the best elements of the Russian system and the sloyd system. Edward P. Seaver, the Boston superintendent of schools described the work of Larsson and his associates:

> The intention of the school committee...is understood to be to continue the experiment for perhaps two years longer, in expectation that there may be a clear demonstration from experience of the best means by which the wants of boys in city grammar schools may be supplied, whether by the Russian shop-work or by the Swedish sloyd, or by some combination and outgrowth of the two, larger and better than either.[80]

Separate displays assembled by Larsson, Leavitt and Eddy were sent as part of the Boston school exhibit to the Exposition in Chicago. In terms of their content, these displays reflected what many visitors considered to be an essentially unified system of manual training.[81] In fact, what the three displays individually represented was the first gradual step towards a synthesis of the sloyd and Russian methods—one which it was felt was suitable for the needs of the American child.[82]

Larsson's work in particular attracted the attention of educators at the Exposition. It seems that the general opinion held by the educators at the exposition was that the experiments in Boston had produced, through the combination of the Russian and the sloyd methods, a system of manual training that was distinctively suited to the needs of American education.[83] As Dr. H. H. Belfield, the director of the Chicago Manual Training School commented in the discussion held after Larsson's presentation of his work at the International Congress of Education:

> The system just presented to us by Mr. Larsson is a great departure from the Swedish Sloyd which came to us several years ago. In common with many others, I had no hesitation in condemning the system as not adapted to American ideas and conditions. Mr. Larsson has shown courage and pedagogical knowledge in introducing the Swedish models, and insisting upon

drawing and in adding to the tools supplied to the pupils. I welcome Mr. Larsson's system, therefore, as an earnest effort to solve a problem which has occupied our attention for years.[84]

Larsson's work was not without criticism. Calvin Woodward, the main advocate of the Russian system, maintained that the distance between Larsson's method and the Russian system was exceedingly small.[85] Serious criticisms were raised by Woodward concerning the making of useful objects, which was key to the sloyd method. According to Woodward:

When Mr. Larsson's pupil thinks of a dove-tailed joint, he thinks of the bracket which uses it, and he may stop there. The other boy, who has mastered the abstract joint, is directly led to see its use in a dozen constructions which lie all around him. He is the more truly free. Still, as I have already intimated, the interval between these different systems, which to-day are more American than anything else, is so narrow that anyone may step across, and I hope we shall not hesitate to step over and help ourselves to the best that there is on either side.[86]

The exhibits and discussions of manual training at the World's Columbian Exposition were by no means limited simply to the Sloyd and Russian method. Charles Bennett, who at the time was associated with the New York College for the Training of Teachers, demonstrated his group method for organizing the teaching of manual instruction. Essentially, the method involved giving the student the opportunity to select and work on several different projects from a large set of illustrative examples made available to him by the instructor. Certain elementary projects were required of each student, as well as supplementary exercises for the more skilled students. Class instruction was provided for the basic projects, while individual instruction was given for the supplementary work.[87] Bennett's method, although developed independently, incorporated many of the same principles developed by Eddy in his classes at Boston, which were also on display at the World's Columbian Exposition.[88]

The exhibits and discussions which focused on the manual training movement at the World's Columbian Exposition represent a continuation of the development of new ideas and methods that began with the introduction of the Russian system of manual training at the Philadelphia Centennial Exposition in 1876. Unlike Philadelphia, where the Russian system was introduced as a totally new system, the exhibit of sloyd methods and materials at the World's Columbian Exposition was not the first introduction of these materials into the United States. The importance of the exhibit was that it brought the sloyd materials and methods to the attention of educators, and demonstrated how the sloyd method could be adopted to the needs of America and be eventually combined with the then dominant Russian system of manual training. According to Richard Waterman, Jr., the presentation and comparison of the Russian and sloyd methods at the exposition:

> ...resulted in a better understanding of each by the supporters of the other, and a conviction that the most successful system would be a combination of the best features of both Russian and Swedish. The American delegates felt so strongly the need for a frequent repetition of these profitable sessions that they took steps to form a National Organization of Manual training Teachers, whose aim would be to provide an opportunity for all the teachers in this field of work to make frequent comparison between their own methods and results and those obtained in other American schools. they would thus be able to profit by the experience gained in many different schools, and to work out, more quickly and surely, the system of Manual Training best adapted to American condition.[89]

The successful combination of these two methods into a new system would not be complete for several years. Yet despite this, as evidenced by the display of manual and industrial arts at the St. Louis Louisiana Purchase exposition in 1904, it would only take a few years for the sloyd and Russian systems to be thoroughly integrated to become a distinctively American system of manual and industrial training.

* * *

As part of the "Addresses of Welcome" that were included in the International Congress of Education, Charles G. Bonney, president of the World's Congress Auxiliary, explained how: "The educational systems of the past have been outgrown."[90] According to him:

> The new education, extended as it will be throughout the world, will do as much as, if not more than, any other agency to promote the unity and peace of mankind.[91]

The educational exhibits at the World's Columbian Exposition described not only the conditions of schooling throughout the United States and much of the world, but also presented a vision of progress linked to knowledge that was to continue as a theme at the 1904 Louisiana Purchase Exposition. It was a vision that reflected a symbolic universe constructed by a group of cultural and educational elites who equated knowledge with power, and the expansion of public schooling, as part of an inevitable march of progress and civilization.

Notes

1. "The Significance of the Frontier in American History," in *The Early Writings of Frederick Jackson Turner, with a List of All His Works Compiled by Everett E. Edwards and an introduction by Fulmer Mood* (Madison, WI: University of Wisconsin Press, 1938), p. 186. For background on the importance of Turner's work see "The Myth of the Garden and Turner's Frontier Hypothesis," pp. 250-260 in Henry Nash Smith's, *Virgin Land: The American West as Symbol and Myth* (Cambridge, MA: Harvard University Press, 1950).
2. Following the Centennial Exhibition in Philadelphia, the Smithsonian Institution participated in numerous local and international expositions including the International Fisheries Exhibitions in Berlin and London (1880 and 1883), the Boston Foreign Exhibition (1883), the Chicago Railway Exhibition (1883), the International Electrical Exhibition in Philadelphia (1884), the Southern Exposition in Louisville (1884), Cincinnati's Industrial Exposition (1884), the World's Cotton Industrial and Cotton Exposition at New Orleans (1885), the Minneapolis Industrial Exposition (1887), the Marietta, Ohio, Exposition (1889), the Paris Exposition (1889), the Patent Centennial (1891) and the Columbian Historian Exhibition in Madrid (1892). See: Robert W. Rydell, *All the World's a Fair: Visions of Empire at American International Expositions, 1876-1916* (Chicago: University of Chicago Press, 1984), p. 43.
3. For background on G. Brown Goode see: Edward P. Alexander, *Museum Masters: Their Museums and Their Influence* (Nashville, TN: The American Association for State and Local History, 1983), Chapter 10, "George Brown Goode and the Smithsonian Museums: A National Museum of Cultural History," pp. 277-310.
4. United States National Museum, *Annual Report* (1896-97), (A Memorial to George Brown Goode) (Washington, DC: U.S. Government Printing Office, 1897), p. 197.
5. *Report of the U.S. National Museum under the Direction of the Smithsonian Institution for the Year Ending June 30, 1891*, G. Brown Goode, "First Draft of a System of Classification for the World's Columbian Exposition," p. 656.
6. *Ibid.*, p. 654.
7. Rydell, *op. cit.*, p. 2.
8. Henry Adams, *The Education of Henry Adams* (New York: The Modern Library, 1931), p. 467.
9. *Ibid.*, p. 341.
10. *Ibid.*, p. 342.
11. Rydell, *op. cit.*, p. 46.
12. Rydell, *op. cit.*, p. 46.

13 Quoted by Rydell, *op. cit.*, p. 46.
14 *Ibid.*, p. 46.
15 The educational displays for the various states tended to be highly repetitious in nature. Like the educational exhibits at the Philadelphia Centennial Exhibition, they typically included extensive portfolios of student work, compilations of educational statistics and photographs of schools. The content of these exhibits can be easily reconstructed by looking at the various reports on the exhibits that were submitted after the Fair. See, for example: *Catalog of Connecticut Educational Exhibit* (No publishing Information, 1893); Howard J. Rogers, "Report on the New York Educational Exhibit," *Report of the Board of General Managers of the Exhibit of the State of New York at the World's Columbian Exposition* (Albany, NY: James B. Lyon, State Printer, 1894), pp. 451–473; and *Sixty-Second Annual Report of the Massachusetts Board of Education: Together with the Sixty-Second Annual Report of the Secretary of the Board, 1897–1898.* (Boston: Wright & Potter Printing Co., State Printers, 1899), pp. 204–294.
16 John Eaton, "The Exhibit of Education at the Columbian Exposition," *Report of the Commissioner of Education for the Year 1892–93*, Vol. 1 (Washington, DC: Government Printing Office, 1895), p. 446.
17 *Ibid.*, p. 452.
18 John Winthrop, *Papers*, A. B. Forbes, ed. (Boston: Massachusetts Historical Society, 1931), Vol. II, p. 295.
19 *Ibid.*, p. 453.
20 *Ibid.*, p. 454.
21 Denton J. Snider, *World's Fair Studies*, Number Two, The Organization of the Fair (Chicago: Chicago Kindergarten College, no date), p. 23.
22 Rydell, *op.cit.*, p. 235.
23 *Ibid.*, p. 40.
24 *Ibid.*, p. 236.
25 *Ibid.*, p. 55.
26 Ibid., p. 56.
27 Quoted by Rydell, *op. cit.*, p. 65.
28 *Ibid.*, p. 56.
29 *Ibid.*, p. 57.
30 Rydell, *op.cit.*, p. 69.
31 Eaton, *op. cit.*, p. 447.
32 Rydell, *op.cit.*, pp. 40–41.
33 Robert A. Trennert, "Fairs, Expositions, and the Changing Image of Southwestern Indians, 1876–1904," *New Mexico Historical Review*, 62, no. 2, April 1987, p. 127.

34 *Ibid.*, p. 134.
35 Quoted by Frederick E. Hoxie, *A Final Promise: The Campaign to Assimilate the Indians, 1880–1920* (Lincoln: University of Nebraska Press, 1984), p. 89.
36 *Ibid.*, p. 89.
37 *Ibid.*, p. 89.
38 *Ibid.*
39 Richard Henry Pratt, *Battlefield and Classroom: Four Decades with the American Indians, 1867–1904*, edited with an introduction by Robert M. Utley (New Haven, CT: Yale University Press, 1964), p. 295.
40 *Ibid.*, p. 303.
41 *Ibid.*
42 *Ibid.*, pp. 304–305.
43 Quoted by Judy Elise Braun, *The North American Indian Exhibits at the 1876 and 1893 World Expositions: The Influence of Scientific Thought Upon Popular Attitudes* (Master's thesis George Washington University, 1975), p. 68.
44 *Ibid.*
45 Quoted by Rydell, *op.cit.*, pp. 63–64.
46 Stephen Waetzoldt, "The School System of the United States," *Report of the Commissioner of Education for the Year 1892–93*, Vol. 1 (Washington, DC: Government Printing Office, 1895), p. 559.
47 Emil Hausknect, "The American System of Education," *Report of the American Commissioner of Education, 1892–93*, p. 522.
48 Jules Violle, "The Chicago Exposition and American Science," *Report of the American Commissioner of Education, 1892–93*, p. 595.
49 National Education Association of the United States, *Proceedings of the International Congress of Education of the World's Columbian Exposition, Chicago, July 25–28, 1893* (New York: National Education Association, 1895), p. iii.
50 *Ibid.*, p. iv.
51 Throughout the Fair, as well as during the Educational Congress, elementary and secondary school teachers from around the country were brought to see the exhibits. Housing was provided by the Woman's dormitory Association, as well as the School-House Dormitory Committee which provided housing for female schoolteachers visiting the Fair. See: Virginia Grant Darney, "Women and World's Fairs: American International Expositions, 1876–1904." Doctoral dissertation, Emory University, 1982, p. 84.
52 *Ibid.*, William Torrey Harris, "Report of the Committee of Arrangements, National Education Association of the International Congress of Education," p. 26.
53 *Ibid.*, James B. Angell, "Second General Session, Tuesday July 25th, 8 O'clock P.M.," p. 34.

54 Ibid., G. W. Ross, "Address," p. 43.
55 Ibid., M. Ergraff Kovalevsky, "Address," p. 56.
56 William Torrey Harris noted prior to the opening of the Exposition in Chicago concerning the importance of bringing together educators on an international basis that:
> It is impossible to estimate the advantages that would result from the mere establishment of personal acquaintances and friendly relations among the leaders of the intellectual and moral world, who now, for the most part, know each other only through the interchange of publication, and perhaps the formalities of correspondence.

See Harris, untitled paper read before the Department of Superintendence of the National Education Association, Brooklyn, New York, February 16, 1892. Included in the William Torrey Harris papers, Missouri Historical Society, St. Louis, Missouri.
57 Stephen Waetzoldt, "The Educational Exhibit in Chicago and the School System of the United States," *Report of the Commissioner of Education for the Year 1892–93*, Vol. I (Washington, DC: Government Printing Office, 1895), p. 556.
58 Ibid., p. 447.
59 Darney, op. cit., p. 84.
60 Ibid., p. 85. In addition to Darney's work, background on the Women's exhibits is provided by Jeanne Madeline Weimann, *The Story of the Woman's Building, World's Columbian Exposition, Chicago 1893* (Chicago: Academy Chicago, 1981).
61 Darney, op. cit., p. 86.
62 Richard Waterman, Jr., "Educational Exhibits at the Columbian Exposition (I), *Educational Review*, 6, October 1893, p. 274.
63 Waetzoldt, op. cit., p. 558.
64 James W. Sanders, *The Education of an Urban Minority: Catholics in Chicago, 1935–1965* (New York: Oxford University Press, 1977).
65 Ibid., p. 133.
66 P. J. Muldoon, editor, *The World's Columbian Catholic Congresses and Educational Exhibit* (Chicago: J. S. Hyland & Company, 1893, n. p.
67 Ibid
68 Ibid., p. 69.
69 Ibid., n.p.
70 Ibid., p. 15.
71 J. H. Trybom, "Sloyd as an Educational Subject," *Proceedings of the National Education Association*, 31, 1892, p. 456.
72 Charles Bennett, *History of Manual and Industrial Education 1870–1917* (Peoria, Illinois: The Manual Arts Press, 1937), pp. 53–106 (Chapter II) includes a complete description of the sloyd method and its history.

73 Ibid., p. 55.
74 Salmon's debt to Cygnaeus is outlined in his work *Slojskolan och Folksskolan* (Gothenburg, 1882), which was translated and included in the *Second Report of the Royal Commissioners on Technical Instruction* (London, 1884). A selection from this translation is included in Bennett, op. cit., pp. 103-105.
75 Gustaf Larson, "Sloyd for Elementary Schools Contrasted with the Russian System of Manual Training," *Proceedings of the National Education Association* (International Congress of Education), Vol. 32, 1893, pp. 600-601. Also see Bennett, op. cit., pp. 67-68, and Tryborn, op. cit., p. 458.
76 Bennett, op. cit., p. 67.
77 Larsson, op. cit., p. 602.
78 See for example: "Manual Training in the Common Schools," Special Report of a Committee of the Board of education in Massachusetts, *Forty-Sixth Annual Report of the Massachusetts Board of Education, 1881-82*, reprinted by Bennett, op. cit., pp. 459-462.
79 Ibid., p. 431.
80 *Reports of the Commission Appointed to Investigate the Existing Systems of Manual Training and Industrial Education* (State of Massachusetts, 1893), pp. 22-23. As quoted by Bennett, op. cit., p. 434.
81 Ibid.
82 Larsson's work was largely based upon the sloyd method while Leavitt and Eddy's used the Russian system as a model. For an outline of their methods with accompanying illustrations see the discussion section appended to Vergil G. Curtis's article "Wood-Work in Grammar Grades," *Proceedings of the National Educational Association*, 1894, pp. 261-267 ("Discussion," pp. 267-278).
83 Bennett, op. cit., p. 434.
84 "Discussion," appended to Larsson, op. cit., p. 605.
85 Ibid.
86 Ibid., p. 606.
87 Bennett, op. cit., p. 434.
88 Bennett, op. cit., p. 438.
89 Richard Waterman, Jr., "International Education Congresses of 1893," *Education*, 6, September 1893, p. 162.
90 "Addresses of Welcome," (International Congress of Education), *Proceedings of the International Congress of Education*, op. cit., p. 17.
91 Ibid., p. 20.

Chapter 4
The Louisiana Purchase Exposition

"Ready to Admit the World," Howard J. Rogers, Chief of the Department
of Education at the Louisiana Purchase Exposition,
cover of the *School Board Journal*, 24, no. 5, May 1904.

In *The Education of Henry Adams*, Henry Adams described the "new American "that had come into being by the beginning of the twentieth century as "the child of steam and the brother of dynamo."[1] Adams believed that a new consciousness—one based upon a pervasive, new technology—had come into being in the years between the closing of the 1876 Philadelphia Centennial Exhibition and the opening of the 1904 St. Louis Louisiana Purchase Exposition. With the new national consciousness came a new American, who:

> ...like the new European was the servant of the powerhouse, as the European of the twelfth century was servant of the Church...[2]

According to Adams, the Louisiana Purchase Exposition was a manifestation of this new power. As he explained:

> The St. Louis Exposition was its first creation in the twentieth century, and for that reason acutely interesting. One saw here a third-rate town of half-a-million people without history, education, unity, or art, and with little capital—without even an element of natural interest except the river which it studiously ignored—but doing what London, Paris, or New York would have shrunk from attempting.[3]

Adams observed that with the exposition in St. Louis a new social order had been created solely by this new power.[4] For the few short months that the Exposition was held "education found new forage" and a "phantasm" as marvelous as any the world had ever observed was created[5]

As was the case with the earlier expositions held in Philadelphia and Chicago, the theme of "knowledge and power"—and the logical corollary of education and progress—was repeatedly emphasized by the organizers of the Fair. Howard Rogers, the director of the educational exhibits at the Exposition, summarized the theme as succinctly as anyone when he said that "the history of human progress is based upon education."[6]

The idea that power in the twentieth century would depend upon knowledge, and that progress was an outcome of that power, was an idea that was fully realized at the Exposition in St. Louis. As Frank Webster Smith argued just prior to its opening, the Exposition enforced the ideal of progress:[7]

> A great exposition is a great educational opportunity. It touches education in many ways and on many sides. It brings together vast collections of facts which furnish unique facilities for observation and information.[8]

Through an exposition:

> ...new relations may be discovered and new facts begin to be. Two powers are thus manifest, the power to present or "expose" facts and the power to influ-

ence and modify ideas and ideals. An exposition is therefore in all its parts educational.[9]

Despite this awareness of the educational potential of the expositions, it was not until the 1904 St. Louis Purchase Exposition that education became the focal point around which an exposition was organized. The Paris Exposition of 1900 had, it should be noted, given education first place in the general classification of the exhibits outlined by the Commissioner General of the Exposition, Monsieur Picard, who believed that education was the source of all human progress.[10] It was not until the Exposition in St. Louis, however, that education was the keynote around which all the exhibits of the Exposition were developed. The director of exhibits, Frederick J. Skiff, explained prior to the opening of the St. Louis Fair that:

> Education will be the keynote of the Universal Exposition of 1904. It is designed to teach all—but primarily and distinctively, as previously stated, the expert working citizenship of the country and the world in all areas of human activities. Each department of the world's labor and development is to be presented at St. Louis, classified and installed in such a manner that all engaged in or interested in such branch of activity may come and see, examine, study and go away advised. Each of the separate sections of the Exposition will be an equivalent of, rather will be in actuality a comprehensive and most effective lesson in the line of industrial progress and social progress which it has been organized to present.[11]

The Palace of Education at the Louisiana Purchase Exposition. Courtesy of the Library of Congress.

The organizers of the Exposition conceived of education in its broadest sense, as education:

> ...which comes to people from observing art and architecture in heroic models, from inspecting exhibits grouped with regard to their dependence and relation to each other, and from seeing processes in connection with the exhibits which will take raw material and transform it, under the eyes of the waiting crowd into the product ready for the market.[12]

The intention was to "establish a clearing house for suggestive ideas whose influence will be carried to every corner of the globe."[13] While many well-known people, from Theodore Roosevelt to Josiah Royce and Woodrow Wilson, commented on the educational significance of the Exposition, perhaps the guiding spirit behind the Exposition was most clearly expressed in a speech delivered by Helen Keller on October 18, 1904:

Cavalry and the crowds at the Louisiana Purchase Exposition. Courtesy of the Library of Congress.

> The Louisiana Purchase Exposition is a great manifestation of all the forces of enlightenment and all of man's thousand torches burn together. The value of everything here and of all is educational. The Exposition is what its distinguished founder intended it to be—a world's university.... All that is gathered here symbolizes the will of the American people that a way shall be paved to the education of all, no matter how humble or limited their capacity.[14]

The importance of education in the general plan of the Exposition was made obvious by the location and space allotted to the Palace of Education. The Louisiana Purchase Exposition was the first of the international expositions to assign a separate building exclusively to educational displays. Even at the Paris Exposition of 1900, the educational display had been in a wing of the Liberal Arts Building. At the Louisiana Purchase Exposition, the Palace of Education, in which most of the educational exhibits were displayed, was located at the very center of activity. Standing on the east side of the Grand Basin, it was close to the Cascades and the Terrace of States. Described as being of the "Corinthian order of Modern Classic Architecture," the palace was built in the shape of an irregular pentagon.[15] It was designed by the St. Louis firm of Eames and Young and cost $350,000 to build. A fifty-foot-high colonnade, topped by a ten-foot cornice, ran around the outside of the entire building. Including the area within the colonnade, the building covered 293,000 square feet, or approximately seven acres with 156,670 feet allocated for exhibits. Of this, forty-three percent of the available space was eventually devoted to foreign exhibits and fifty-seven percent to displays from the United States.[16]

Statuary related to the exhibit surrounded the building and was placed throughout the colonnade and interior. Almost all of the pieces displayed on the facade were executed by the St. Louis sculptor Robert P. Bringhurst and included such subjects as the "Thread of Fate," "Geography," "Music," and "Manual Training." At the northern end of the building stood a statue of the Swiss educator Pestalozzi by A. Jaegers, while at the western end was a bust of Horace Mann executed by H. K. Bush-Brown.[17]

The object of the educational exhibit was twofold: to present a comprehensive view of educational progress in the United States, and to draw attention to those foreign countries which had developed unusual or particularly successful systems of education. The development of the exhibit was probably a direct outgrowth of the United States display at the Paris Exposition of 1900. As Howard Rogers explained in his final report:

> From the favorable comments which had been made upon the Educational Exhibit of the United States Commission at the Paris Exposition of 1900

both in foreign and domestic journals, a discussion had arisen concerning the relative merits of the different systems of education in various nations, and it was felt that more thorough comparisons could be made from the St. Louis exhibits. That the theory of public education in Europe was different from that in this country was an admitted premise. Whether each was best adapted to the conditions underlying its own national development; whether each contained methods that could be advisedly adapted to the system of the other; whether the tendencies of the two were more widely or less sharply divergent than formerly; and whether conclusions could be drawn clearly as to which has the most beneficial effect on the commercial and industrial development of the country, were the larger problems for which the educational exhibit was to furnish the solution.[18]

Nations and colonies from every quarter of the globe were invited by the directors of the Exposition to participate in the educational exhibit. Argentina, Austria, Belgium, Bulgaria, Canada, Ceylon, China, Cuba, France, Germany, Great Britain, Hungary, Italy, Japan, Mexico, Monaco, Nicaragua, Portugal, Rumania, Siam, Spain, Sweden and Syria were among those who submitted displays.[19]

The Education Exhibit was planned by the organizers of the Exposition with the assumption that the twentieth century would experience very different needs in education than did the nineteenth century. Whereas colonialism had dominated international politics during the Eighteenth and nineteenth centuries, commercial and industrial affairs were seen as playing an increasing role during the twentieth century. At a meeting held by the directors of the Exposition concerning the construction of the Palace of Education, for example, the following comment was made concerning the problem of education and its relationship to the Fair:

> No subject is of such vital interest to the nations, is engrossing so much the attention of cabinets and ministries at the present time as education, owing to the industrial and commercial activity and the reciprocal relations of labor and capital, all of which are vitally affected by the educational system of a country.[20]

Similar ideas were expressed throughout much of the publicity written for the Exposition. In an article published while the Fair was underway, Howard Rogers speculated that:

> The twentieth century will be noted for the struggle between nations for commercial and industrial supremacy. At times an appeal to arms will be made

because of a clash of interests, but the nations who will win, and who will control the trade of the world will be those who train their future citizens from the standpoint of efficiency. The test which will establish the higher efficiency will be that of success; and the nation whose system of education gives to its citizens breadth of observation, power of adaption to emergencies, and the ability to do things, will stand preeminent in the educational and commercial world.[21]

The displays in the Palace of Education were intended to show not only what was currently going in education throughout the world, but what could be accomplished in the future as well. There were model classes for the blind, as well as for the deaf and dumb. Children from St. Louis participated in daily class exercises as part of the city's school exhibit. Regular classes were also held in the exhibits of various business colleges. In the displays of the Mechanical and Agricultural Colleges, model hygiene (in addition to physical, chemical and bacteriological) laboratories were in operation for visitors to observe. Daily lectures on pedagogy were part of the German exhibit, and a Berlitz language school ran classes as part of the French educational exhibit. A brief description of one of the classes organized by the St. Louis Public Schools is included in the journal of Edmund Philbert. Describing a conversation that he had with a Chicago man while visiting the Exposition, Philbert wrote that when asked

> ...how the St. Louis Fair compared with Chicago's he hesitated and I said, "You don't want to go back on Chicago." "Oh, it isn't that," he said, "Now you take this place right here, and you have Chicago beat to death, its a beautiful sight at night. I went through the Educational Building first and saw beautiful transparencies in the California University exhibit. They were large pictures, about sixteen by eighteen inches of the moon, eclipses, meteors, buildings, trees, etc. I saw boys from the St. Louis public schools doing bench work. Each boy had a bench, saw, hammer, chisel, plane, square, etc. and a drawing of the article on which he was working." [22]

As the host city for the Exposition, St. Louis had assembled an extensive exhibit from her public schools. An area measuring approximately 27' x 140' was assigned to the city for its exhibit. The facade of the exhibit consisted of twenty pillars between which archways led into the exhibit itself. On each pillar were transparencies with drawings illustrating the history of education from Ancient to Modern times. The spandrels contained photographs of children from the city's schools participating in classes.[23]

Examples of the children's work from kindergarten through the high school level were exhibited. Models of schools with explanations of their construction and extensive diagrams of the organization of the school system at the city, county and state level were included. Photographs of school buildings and classes from kindergartens to evening classes for adult immigrants were displayed as well.[24]

Probably of greatest interest to most visitors to the Exposition was the actual schoolroom described by Philbert. In a space measuring approximately 27' x 30', kindergarten classes, lessons in manual training and construction, music, science, laboratory instruction, gymnastic instruction, as well as classes for the deaf were held in conjunction with the exhibit.[25]

The St. Louis school exhibit and the Exposition in general, stimulated a great deal of interest and enthusiasm among the members of the St. Louis school board, as well as among local teachers and administrators. In addition, local school children were given numerous opportunities to visit the Exposition. Besides the students who participated as members of the demonstration classes, a total of 70,000 school children attended the Fair under the sponsorship of the schools.

Entrance to the St. Louis Public School Exhibit. Personal collection of the author.

Interior of the St. Louis Public School Exhibit. Personal collection of the author.

Hoping to keep the spirit of the Exposition alive in its schools once the Exposition closed its doors, the superintendent of schools, F. Louis Soldan, and the assistant superintendent, Carl Rathmann, persuaded the School Board to set up an educational museum.[26] In September 1904, the School Board authorized the allotment of $1,000 for the purchase of items from foreign exhibits that could be included in the museum. Purchases included botanical collections, stuffed animals, art objects and a large collection of lantern slides. Important contributions of exhibit materials were made to the schools by countries such as Japan, France, Germany, Australia and New Zealand.[27]

From its inception, "Bring the world to the child" was the museum's motto. It clearly expressed the continuation of the spirit of the Louisiana Purchase Exposition. Just as the Exposition, through its exhibits, had brought the world to St. Louis, the Educational Museum through its exhibits brought the world to the child. By studying artifacts, lantern slides and exhibits, the child could try to bridge the gap between their own world and the real world.[28]

The Educational Museum opened on April 11, 1905. It is commonly recognized as the first audiovisual program established in conjunction with a school system in the United States. Originally located in the Wyman School, the Museum was put under the supervision of Miss Amelia Meissner, who served as its curator from June 1905 until her retirement nearly forty years later.[29]

The Louisiana Purchase Exposition clearly had an important impact on the early organization and development of the museum. Meissner's assignment to the museum, for example, was a direct result of her work as a photographer for the St. Louis school exhibit at the Exposition.[30] The Exposition was also important in convincing teachers within the school system of the value of using "hands-on materials" in teaching their children. As Assistant Superintendent Rathman explained concerning the teachers:

> Their excursions to the World's Fair with their classes had shown them what a powerful stimulus the observations of the wealth of real things from all parts of the world had given the children, how boys and girls who had never shown much interest in geography and nature work had become wide-awake and eager to learn. They readily saw the value of museum collections, arranged in accordance with the course of study and affording a means of systematic and efficient illustration of all school work.[31]

According to Rathmann, the use of the museum's collection had a major impact on the character of the school system's curriculum. Instead of simply studying maps and textbooks in geography, for example, the children were given the opportunity to actually handle the raw materials and industrial products of a country. Through the study of photographs and lantern slides they were able to learn about the climate, occupations and products of different countries and people.[32]

The establishment of the Educational Museum of the St. Louis Public Schools, as a direct outgrowth of the Louisiana Purchase Exposition, clearly fulfilled the hope expressed by John Philbrick after the Centennial Exhibition that the expositions would inspire school districts to set up small museums of technology and natural history for their students. This was the beginning of audiovisual and media education in the United States.[33]

Special education played a prominent role in the exhibits at the Louisiana Purchase Exposition. As mentioned earlier, there were model classes for the blind, as well as for the deaf and dumb. While arguments were made for providing "defective" students with as normal an education as possible,[34] for the establishment of laboratory settings for the study of children with special needs,[35] other more unsettling arguments were made as well. Edward Ellis Allen, in an address at the Fair, described how educators in state-sponsored institutions in Kansas had tried a "very radical experiment" in which:

> The operation of castration has been performed on several boys, after which they have been found to be so improved that some were transferred from the custodial to the school department, some sent home.[36]

Much attention was given in the educational exhibits to displaying individuals who had overcome handicaps. Helen Keller, for example, achieved national attention with the speech she gave at the Exposition.[37] In the Kansas model school for the deaf and blind, the "Blind Twins from Kansas" gave violin performances that were extremely popular among the visitors to the Exposition.[38]

As with earlier expositions, visitors to the Louisiana Purchase Exposition were given an opportunity to see extensive displays sponsored by the Smithsonian Institution. In June of 1902 Congress allocated $1,250,000 for government buildings and exhibits, which included the Smithsonian.[39]

Delivery wagon for the Educational Museum of the St. Louis Public Schools, c. 1906. Personal collection of the author.

The Smithsonian Exhibit at the Louisiana Purchase Exposition. Courtesy of the Smithsonian Institution.

The government building contained a total floor space of 102,000 square feet. A total of 16,500 square feet of this space was assigned to the Smithsonian. In addition to exhibits from the Hodgkins fund, the Astrophysical Observatory, the Children's Room, the Bureau of Ethnology and the National Museum, an area immediately outside of the Government Building was devoted to an exhibit of the National Zoological Park, which was under the supervision of the Smithsonian.[40]

The main exhibit for the Smithsonian included a complete set of publications for the Institution, a quarter-size model of the Langley gas-driven aerodrome of 1904 and the 1896 steam-driven Langley aerodrome, a cast of the bronze tablet which had been placed on James Smithson's grave in Genoa, Italy, as well as numerous photographs of the Institution and its secretaries.[41]

A nearly exact replica of the Children's Room occupied the main aisle of the exhibit. The Children's Room, which had first opened in 1888, included extensive exhibits of live and stuffed animals.[42] Exhibit materials included discussions of how animals camouflage themselves, as well as examples of interesting minerals and butterflies.[43]

The exhibit of the Astrophysical Observatory included extensive displays of instrumentation. Of greatest interest to most visitors was the two-mirrored coelostat, a telescopic device which made it possible to observe the reflected image of the sun in a darkened room.[44]

At previous expositions the exhibits of the Smithsonian's National Zoological Park was limited to pictures and models of the buildings and various photographs. At St. Louis, it was decided to develop an extensive exhibit of live birds that were housed in what was probably the largest flight cage that had been built up until that time, measuring 228 feet long, 84 feet wide and 50 feet high. A central arched passage traversed the entire length of the exhibit, making it possible for visitors to actually walk through the center of the flight cage and observe birds as diverse as wild geese, trumpeter swans, Cuban flamingos, roseate spoonbills, various species of ibis, herons, cranes, pelicans, cormorants, vultures, canaries, Javan sparrows, bullfinches, goldfinches and linnets—to name just a few.[45]

The Louisiana Purchase Exposition included the largest Anthropological exhibit of any of the world's fairs held up until that time. The directors of the exhibit had as their purpose to establish:

> ...a comprehensive anthropological exhibition, constituting a Congress of Races, and exhibiting particularly the barbarous and semi-barbarous peoples of the world, as nearly as possible in their ordinary and native environments.[46]

The Anthropological Exhibit was placed under the direction of W. J. McGee. McGee had previously achieved national recognition as the ethnologist-in-charge of the Bureau of American Ethnology. Although forced out of his position at the Bureau because of financial irregularities, he nonetheless remained a major figure in anthropological studies in the United States.[47]

McGee outlined his theories on racial progress in a series of addresses given in 1899. The first, entitled "The Trend of Human Progress," was delivered before the Washington Academy of Sciences and the second, "National Growth and National Character," before the National Geographic Society.[48] In "The Trend of Human Progress," McGee argued for an interpretation of the evolution of human history involving the development from "low to high," from "dullness toward brightness" and from "idleness toward intellectual uprightness." McGee believed that the driving force behind human progress and development was a function of what he termed "cephalization" and "cheirization"—cephalization being the gradual increase of the cranial capacity of different races, and chreirization the systematic increase in manual capacity. Arguing that observation demonstrated that the white race could do more and do it better than the yellow race, and the yellow race more than the black or red races, McGee concluded that as a result of cephalization and cheirization culture advanced along lines of racial achievement.[49]

McGee's lecture before the Washington Academy of Sciences and the National Geographic Society provided an interpretation in which racial progress was made synonymous with industrial progress.[50] When McGee arrived in St. Louis in August of 1903 to begin to organize the Anthropological Exhibit, he made it clear that the exhibits at the Fair would provide a demonstration of his racial theories. According to him:

> The aim of the Department of Anthropology will at the World's Fair will be to represent human progress from the dark prime to the highest enlightenment, from savagery to civic organization, from egoism to altruism.[51]

According to McGee the method employed by the exhibit would be to "...use living peoples in their accustomed avocations as our great object lesson."[52] He placed particular emphasis on the exhibits of the Indian schools at the fair, which he felt represented "America's best effort to elevate the lower races."[53]

A Patagonian family "on exhibit" at the Louisiana Purchase Exposition. Courtesy of the Library of Congress.

Despite cutbacks on funding, by the opening of the fair McGee had converted the western section of the fairgrounds into a massive ethnological display area. Pygmies from Africa, Patagonian "giants" from Argentina, Ainu aborigines from Japan and Kwakiutl Indians from Vancouver Island, as well as various groups of American Indians made up the living ethnological exhibits. Separate, but adjacent to McGee's ethnological exhibit was the United States government exhibit of approximately 1,200 Filipinos confined to a "reservation" covering forty-seven acres.[54]

Support for a special Philippine Exhibit was evident early in the planning for the Fair. Besides providing an exhibit of the conditions and people in the Philippines, the exhibit was perceived by many as contributing to bringing the former Spanish colony under American control. Future president William Howard Taft, as the civil governor of the Philippines, for example, commented that he believed that the proposed Philippine Exhibit would have a "moral effect" on the Philippine natives and would have a positive effect on their pacification. President Theodore Roosevelt and Elihu Root, the secretary of war, both encouraged efforts to organize the exhibit.[55]

William Howard Taft, first civilian governor-general of the Philippines, and foreign dignitaries entering the Philippine Educational Building at the Louisiana Purchase Exposition. Courtesy of the Library of Congress.

The Philippine "reservation" was described by William P. Wilson, chairman of the United States government's Philippine Exposition Board as being "an exposition within an exposition."[56] It was divided into three cultural spheres: the first depicting the civilizing influence of the Spanish, the second depicting the present ethnological conditions of the islands, and the third depicting the beneficial results that Filipinos and Americans could expect from the United States rule over the islands. At the center of the exhibit were four large Spanish-type buildings, including an upper-class residence, a government building, an educational building and a reproduction of the commercial museum in Manila.[57] According to Robert Rydell,

> The pervading imperial message of the reservation was inescapable and apparent from the moment visitors set foot on the forested acreage set aside for the display.[58]

Igorots at the Louisian Purchase Exposition. Courtesy of the Library of Congress.

The ethnological villages that made up the Philippine reservation portrayed a wide-range of Filipinos including Visayans "the high and more intelligent class of natives," the Moros "fierce followers of Mohammed," the Bagabo "savages," "monkey-like" Negritos and "picturesque" Igorots. In addition to the native groups, an encampment of Philippine Scouts and Constabulary numbering nearly 700 were in attendance to police the reservation. These paramilitary forces who were drawn from the "more civilized Filipinos" were seen as demonstrating the results of American rule and were set in deliberate juxtaposition to the relatively primitive Negritos and Igorots.[59]

Racism, however, was even manifested against the members of the Scouts and Constabulary. When they accepted an invitation to tour the exhibits with young white women schoolteachers from St. Louis, they found themselves taunted as "niggers" because of their skin color. During the tour, a number of United States Marines with the exposition's police force, known as the Jefferson guard, threatened to arrest the women for being with "Negroes" and kicked their Filipino escorts to the ground. After the Scouts returned to their camp, a larger group of Marines charged at the Filipinos shooting revolvers in the air and shouting, "Come on boys! Let's clean the Gu-Gus off the earth!"[60]

Under American rule, the Philippines were seen as being led towards a higher plane of civilization. As one commentator after the Fair noted:

> While there is much savagery in the Philippines, there are also perceptible evidences of creditable civilization, and the process of development is proceeding rapidly in many parts of the islands. Manila naturally reflects, as it embodies the best type of Filipino life, because it has for centuries been the entrepot and clearing house of the country's commerce and financial intercourse with other nations.[61]

Cultural development was seen as being synonymous with economic development. As Rydell has pointed out, the Filipino population was perceived as being both "willing workers and consumers in the burgeoning overseas market being established by American commercial interests."[62]

Education played a key role in the plan for social and economic domination of the Philippines. Three years after the first American military troops were landed in the Philippines, seven hundred American teachers were transported there. Serving in a largely advisory capacity, the American teachers quickly made English the main language of instruction throughout the island. American cultural values and traditions superseded those of the previous Spanish colonial administration.[63]

The Philippine educational exhibit reflected the imperial role that the United States assumed in the Philippine's affairs. Installed in a miniature copy of the Manila Cathedral, the exhibit included collections sent by a total of four hundred and thirty-eight exhibitors and consisted of eight thousand five hundred and forty-two separate sets of materials.⁶⁴ A model school was in operation from July 19th to the closing of the Fair. Described as a typical "nipa and bamboo school house arranged for exhibition purposes," it was under the direction of Pilar Zamora—a Tagalog teacher who taught in the Philippine Normal School. Two sessions were held each day except Monday, the first from 9:00 to 10:30 A.M. for children from the Visayan Village, and from 10:30 to 11:30 A.M. for children from the non-Christian tribes. These included children of the Bontoc, Igorot, Suyoc Igorot, Bagobo, Tinguian, Samal, Moro and Lanao Moro tribes. It is interesting to note the separation of Christian and non-Christian students from one another—the supposedly more intelligent and advanced Visayans being kept apart from the more primitive Igorots, Bagobos and Moros.⁶⁵

Tremendous interest was shown in the demonstration classes on the part of visitors to the Fair. Despite only two and a half hours of classes being held a day, the number of visitors observing the classes frequently numbered over 2,000 per day.⁶⁶

At the meeting of the National Educational Association a number of speakers from both the United States and the Philippines spoke about the educational situation in the Philippines and the impact that the Americans were having on them. Throughout these speeches the superiority of the American culture and its people is assumed. E. B. Bryan, a professor in Education and Social Psychology from Indiana University, for example, explained in a speech entitled "Education in the Philippines" that in the case of the Filipinos:

> These people excel in certain things; in certain other things they do not equal the Saxon child. Briefly, these people excel in all things that are based upon memory or imitation.... In the more abstruse thought-work I think I am correct when I say they do not equal the Saxon child.⁶⁷

The schools clearly played a crucial role in affirming the subservient status of the Filipinos to their American overseers. In this context a classic colonial educational model was being put in place.⁶⁸ Evidence of this fact can be seen in a speech delivered for the National Educational Association meeting by Maria Del Pilar Zamora, the teacher for the demonstration school in the Philippine reservation. Explaining that the acceptance of the new American government by the Filipinos was by no means total, Zamora argued that the influence of the schools was seen as a convincing argument for the Filipinos' need to emulate the Americans. As she explained:

> The Filipinos are beginning to realize their needs, and to become Americanized in their thought and in their ambition. The hatred which for some time the Filipinos felt toward the Americans is being replaced by respect and admiration. [69]

In summary, the educational exhibit of the Philippine schools, combined with the ethnological exhibits of the Philippine people, provided a powerful justification and rationale for the United States economic and cultural domination of the Philippines. In doing so, as Robert Rydell argues "the Louisiana Purchase Exposition gave a utopian dimension to American imperialism."[70]

If the Philippine exhibit at the Louisiana Purchase Exposition reflected the United States imperial policy overseas, then the exhibit of Native Americans at the Fair reflected its policy of domination within the confines of its borders. Three separate types of Indian exhibits were included at the Fair. In the Fair's amusement section, known as the "Pike," were to be found shows such as "Cummings Wild West Indian Congress and Rough Riders," the "Cliff Dwellers" (which was an attempt to reconstruct a Pueblo Indian Village) and "Alaska" (which included live Eskimos.) Under the direction of the United States Bureau of Indian Affairs, the Smithsonian Institution's Bureau of American Ethnology and the United States National Museum's Department of Anthropology a second type of exhibit was developed that attempted to provide an interpretation of Indian culture in the United States through a display of traditional artifacts and research materials. The third section of the Indian exhibit displayed various tribal groups in the same way that various native groups had been exhibited as part of the Philippine exhibit. In addition, a model Indian school and exhibit was also set up.[71]

Funding for the Indian exhibit was provided by Congress, which appropriated $40,000 for the exhibit in June of 1902. The purpose of the exhibit was to assemble:

> Such representatives of the different Indian tribes and such exhibits from Indian agencies, schools, archives, as he may deem advisable or necessary to illustrate the past and present conditions of the Indians and Indian tribes of the United States, and the progress made by such in education, art, and industry, and the methods of education and government, and such other matters and things as will fully illustrate Indian advancement in civilization.[72]

The model for the exhibit was drawn directly from the Indian exhibit at the World's Columbian Exposition of 1893.[73] The Indian school exhibit was placed under the direction of S. M. McCowan, who was superintendent of the Chilocco Industrial School in Oklahoma. Early in the spring of 1903 McCowan came to

St. Louis to work on the exhibit. His purpose was to show the "native arts and industries" by which the various Indian groups lived, and to show the "process and methods of their ethnological and industrial evolution."[74]

Under McCowen's supervision a two-story school building measuring 40 by 208 feet was built. Eventually several hundred Indians were brought to the Fair including members of the Kickapoo, Maricopa, Navajo, Arapaho, Cheyenne, Pawnee, Wichita, Apache, Pueblo (Sandra Clara and Acoma), Jicarilla, and Chippewa tribes. Building materials were brought to the Exposition by the various tribes so that they could construct authentic dwellings for themselves.[75]

The Indian school building and its exhibits opened on June 1, 1904. On the first day alone, 10,000 visitors passed through the exhibit. Old and new were deliberately contrasted in the exhibit. Surrounding the Indian school was a semi-circle of hogans, tepees and other traditional native constructed dwellings. There were sixteen booths inside the building where the Indians carried out traditional crafts. These included Navajo blanket weaving, Jicarilla Apache basket making and Wichita, Pawnee and Cheyenne bead and buckskin work. Among the most interesting of the living exhibits was the Indian Chief Geronimo, who was given a booth of his own in which he made bows and arrows which he sold along with photographs of himself.[76]

Group of Indians in front of St. Louis Indian School. World's Fair 1904. Courtesy of the Smithsonian Institution.

Juxtaposed to the traditional dwellings and exhibits of Indians at work on traditional crafts, were the exhibits with students from schools such as Chilocco, Haskell, Genoa, Fort Shaw and Sacton demonstrating work in domestic and industrial arts such as printing, cooking, wheelwrighting and harness making.[77]

The contrast of old and new, of the progress from primitive culture to civilization, was a theme that was deliberately emphasized in the design of the exhibit. It was a theme that was clearly picked up by visitors to the exhibit. At the opening of the meeting of the Department of Indian Education for the National Educational Association, A. M. Dockery, the Governor of Misouri, commented that:

> Here on these grounds are ample evidences of progress. Over in the Indian congress, and in some of the attractions of the Pike, many an old chief takes pride in exhibiting the Indian of the plain and forest. In these buildings, however, the descendants of these same tribes are as jealous of the culture attained by your efforts as were the denizens of the woods of their prowess with bow and arrow or the repeating rifle. Both have reason to be proud. The original inhabitants of these great American lands were lords of all. Having yielded to our government, the older ones still glory in the traditions of their forefathers, and their fealty is to be commended. The tribal youth too, are proud of their ancestry, but have been taught in the schools until they now see the advantages of the highest civilization and are quick to respond to it.[78]

Fierce and once feared warriors such as Geronimo having been pacified, could now be exhibited as curiosities for visitors to the Fair. Lip service was paid to the traditions of their culture as Indian youths adopted the education and technology of what was perceived as a superior culture.

Tradition could be dealt with, but only if it was perceived as being part of a largely abandoned past. As Calvin Woodward, director of the Manual Training School at Washington University and perhaps the most prominent leader in the field of industrial education explained:

> Believe me, most of the civilization of today stands upon what I might very properly call a technical foundation. And the civilization of the Indians is to be built upon a technical foundation. They must understand the laws of industrial progress. They must not bring in too much of tradition. While I ask no Indian to forget his father and mother, or to speak disrespectfully of his people, I do ask him to receive graciously and openly what the new civilization has to offer. When we reach out our hands to lift him up to a higher standard, we do not do it with any scorn or contempt of the past. I would have them build upon the past a noble future. You have been told of the triumphs of this generation. You can hardly realize how completely mechanical force and nature-force have taken the place of muscular men and women.[79]

The Louisiana Purchase Exposition 119

Geronimo and seven other Apache men, women and a boy posed in front of tents at the Louisiana Purchase Exposition, St. Louis. Courtesy of the Library of Congress.

Of the foreign displays related to commercial and industrial education, none was as extensive as that of Germany. Placing particular emphasis upon the growth of technical high schools in their country, the German exhibitors were particularly interested in demonstrating how their educational system trained individuals for technical professions as well as for positions in business and the civil service.[80]

> One of the rooms devoted exclusively to the German technical high school contained an extensive display on methods used to train individuals for the colonial service. It included thorough studies of the geography and typography of different colonies and foreign countries in which Germans might find themselves serving; the major trade routes with those areas; and their fertile and unproductive regions. Detailed descriptions were given of mineral resources, as well as the animal and plant life of the particular regions being studied. All of this was included in the normal curriculum of the school, so that when an agent of either a German firm or the government went to a colony or foreign country, he was familiar with it as possible.[81]

Similar displays emphasizing commercial and industrial development were set up by France and Belgium, while manual training was particularly emphasized in the Swedish, Italian and Austrian exhibits. None of these displays, however, was as extensive as that of Germany.

The lack of a commercial and industrial focus in the American displays was criticized at length by German visitors to the Exposition. In a report submitted to the State Department by the American Consul-General in Berlin, Mr. Mann, it was explained that various German visitors to the Fair felt that the exhibit presented by the United States showed little innovation.

It was not, however, the lack of emphasis upon technical training in the American schools which was most astonishing to for German visitors to the Exposition, but rather the insufficient training in commercial fields offered in the American schools. Mann's report continues:

> Most surprising of all appeared to the German visitors the absence of any adequate system of special education for commerce, banking and foreign trade. Reduced to the simplest terms these investigators generally conclude the reliance on a general and more or less superficial education, together with natural adaptability, to fit young men for almost every walk in life, and the lack of specialized study in physical science, modern languages and the industrial arts will, if persisted in, neutralize much of the advantages which our country enjoys through natural resources and advantageous geographical position for the South American, Mexican and Asiatic trade.[82]

Probably the main idea which came out of the foreign exhibits was the subordination in the displays erected by nearly all of the industrial nations of the humanities to commercial, industrial and manual training. Significantly, this was not a phenomenon limited to Europe's industrialized nations. Japan, for example, presented exhibits which emphasized its increasing industrial development. Extensive statistical charts showed the growth of the country's educational system since the introduction of Western methods in 1867; displays included everything from new methods for identifying criminals, to the basic outlines of elementary education in Japan and the teaching of the blind and physically handicapped.[83]

Compared with the foreign exhibits, the displays from the United States show a remarkable uniformity. After visiting the Palace of Education Edward Schniederhahn, a St. Louisian, noted that: "The public school exhibits were largely a repetition, one of the other..."[84] The similarity of the educational exhibits displayed by the different American states and cities was commented on by a number of people at the time. A total of thirty-four states and territories, four cities and numerous technical and professional schools, universities, colleges and art schools presented exhibits. Howard Rogers felt that the similarity of the exhibits was indicative of an important tendency towards a unified system of education throughout the United States. In his final report as the director of the Department of Education Rogers stated that:

> If it were asked why the education of forty-five states, each under a separate, independent government, separated by tradition, clime and culture, show such unity, I would assert that it is due to two causes: first to the United States Bureau of Education, under the able guidance of its great chief, Dr. William T. Harris; and, second to the influence of the National Education Association. The Bureau of Education cannot arbitrarily shape the policy of any state or section, but so wisely has the power of suggestion been used, so forcibly has the inference from statistic been drawn, and so clearly has the comparison of systems, foreign and domestic, been set forth, that our educational policies from east to west have by the force of logic formed in parallel columns.[85]

The importance of the National Education Association in shaping the exhibits of the various American states at the Louisiana Purchase Exposition cannot be overemphasized. As early as June of 1901, the Association had appointed a committee to coordinate the work of various school districts throughout the country in setting up displays. Nearly all of the superintendents from the larger cities in the East and the Midwest were members. The committee also included such leading educational figures as William T. Harris (Chairman), F. Louis Soldan, Nicholas Murray Butler, William R. Harper and Calvin M. Woodward.[86]

Undoubtedly the highlight of the Exposition in relationship to education was the International Congress on Education, which was held in conjunction with the regular annual meeting of the National Education Association. Delegates for the congress were drawn from around the world, as well as from the United States. Among its purposes were to discuss: 1. the organization and administration of educational systems throughout the world; 2. methods for the preparation and certification of teachers; 3. the adoption of the educational systems of different countries to conform with their commercial and industrial needs; and 4. the status of educational systems throughout the world as indicated by their displays at the Exposition.[87]

David Francis, the president of the Louisiana Purchase Exposition Company, in opening remarks to those attending the International Congress of Education emphasized the role that education had played from the earliest planning stages for the Exposition. According to him, the

...educational motive has followed this enterprise from its beginning... The management of the Exposition has been claiming, and I think not entirely without grounds that this Exposition is a university in itself. We feel that its educational benefit far surpasses its material force. We have classified all of the products here exhibited, but this Exposition is not confined to an exhibition of material. We propose to include here not only that which the hand of man has wrought, but the best that his brain has conceived. The intellectual exhibits of the international congresses, that have been arranged in conjunction with this Exposition will in our judgement, be a marker in the thought of the world.[88]

Francis was not only aware of the fact that the international congresses, like the one for education, anticipated the development of international research associations, but that the Louisiana Purchase Exposition might represent the last of the great International Expositions. Commenting on the Louisiana Purchase Exposition, he explained how:

...this Exposition, comprehensive as it is in every line of human endeavor, will, in my judgement, be about the last exposition of this universal character that will be held during this generation at least. I make this prophecy, that these international congresses which have been planned in connection with this Universal Exposition will be the precursor of other international congresses, in which, or thru which, this ambitious effort to demonstrate the unity of all knowledge may be pursued, and may be followed to a successful conclusion.[89]

As had been the case at previous expositions, it was assumed by Francis that one of the major functions of the Exposition would be to make foreign visitors aware of the achievements of industrialized nations such as the United States. In this context education played a crucial role. According to Francis:

Foreign countries are participating to an extent never known before. Why? Because of the curiosity they cherish concerning the people who have made such wonderful progress within so short a period as a century and a third. We tell them that this progress has been achieved because of the universal education of the people of this country. We say to them that, altho we govern ourselves, altho there may be a change in administration, or a change in the policy of this country once in four years, never do we for a moment lose faith in the stability of our institutions; and we cherish this confidence because of the fact that everybody in this country is educated. We think that general education is the very foundation stone of our republican institutions.[90]

Similar comments were made by other speakers welcoming those attending the Congress. William Torrey Harris, repeating themes he had presented at the Philadelphia Centennial Exposition over a quarter of a century earlier, maintained that:

> ...we are here, first of all, to study the Exposition itself; the exposition of the industries of all people; not merely the Industries of the United States, but the industries of Europe, and of South America, and all of all parts of the world. Generous and friendly nations have sent here their results, in order that they may compare them with ours; in order that they may show us their processes of industry, laying great stress upon that; so that it is in a much higher sense an object-lesson that is educative in its character that perhaps any other international expositions that has ever been held. We behold here the results. We have come here with the conviction that the schools have had to do with our industrial success. The school has contributed to this enormous, this colossal, result which we see here.[91]

The educational exhibits were seen as providing a tangible demonstration of the economic and social progress achieved by the American people and their educational system.

> In the exhibit of the Bureau of Education we have brought out the statistics of our national progress, showing by charts the proofs of our rapid growth, and of the completeness with which we are reaching all classes of our population.[92]

* * *

Nearly 10,000 people from around the world registered as participants for the International Congress on Education,[93] while approximately 20,000,000 individuals visited the Exposition during the seven months that it was open to the public.[94] The spirit of the Exposition, and more specifically of its educational exhibits, was perhaps best expressed by David R. Francis at the opening ceremonies for the International Congress of Education. For him the Fair and its exhibits represented:

> ...education which comes to a people from observing art and architecture in heroic models; from observing exhibits in relation to their interdependence upon each other; and from watching processes, in connection with those exhibits, which take the raw product, and under the eyes of the beholder transform it into the finished product, ready for the markets of the world.[95]

Others were more direct in their comments. J. J. Sheppard, the principal of the High School of Commerce in New York stated, for example, that:

> It hardly needs any presentation of data to prove that this is a commercial age and America is a commercial country. It has been well said by one of the most foremost of European statesmen that, as the sixteenth and seventeenth centuries were marked by religious wars, the eighteenth by the development of liberal ideas, and the nineteenth by questions of nationality, so is the twentieth century to be distinguished by the struggle for existence among the nations in the field of commerce.[96]

* * *

In conclusion, the educational exhibits at St. Louis, like their predecessors at Chicago and Philadelphia—and the international expositions in general—were manifestations of a new power and hegemony. Unlike previous ages, it was a hegemony based in technological and scientific advancements—ones often corrupted to serve the purposes of the dominant culture. In this new cultural equation, education and knowledge became an instrument of power. In the final chapter we will examine the significance of this fact in greater detail.

Notes

1 Henry Adams, *The Education of Henry Adams* (New York: The Modern Library, 1931), p. 466.
2 *Ibid.*
3 *Ibid.*
4 *Ibid.*
5 *Ibid.*, p. 467.
6 Howard Rogers, "Education, Its Beginning and Progress," in J. W. Buel, editor, *Louisiana and the Fair*, Vol. VIII (St. Louis: World's Progress Publishing, 1905), p. 2787.
7 Frank Webster Smith, "Education at American Expositions," *Education*, Vol. 24, no. 4, December 1903, p. 231.
8 *Ibid.*, p. 467.
9 *Ibid.*
10 Howard J. Rogers, "Educational Exhibit," *The Universal Exposition of 1904* (St. Louis, 1904), p. 5. This was a regular publication put out at the time of the

Exposition and should not be confused with David R. Francis's history of the Fair published under the same title in 1913.

11 David R. Francis, *The Universal Exposition of 1904* (St. Louis, 1913), p. 55.
12 J. W. Buel, editor, *Louisiana and the Fair: An Exposition of the World, Its People and Their Achievements*, vol. 8 (St. Louis, Missouri: World's Progress Publishing Company, 1905), pp. 1-11. This quotation is taken from the introduction written by Howard J. Rogers.
13 *Ibid.*, p. 2813.
14 Buel, *Fair*, pp. 2890-2891.
15 For a detailed description of the architecture of the Exposition see: George Zolnay, "Architecture at the Exposition," *National Education Association Proceedings* (1904), pp. 167-172.
16 Rogers, "Report," p. 1.
17 Francis, *Universal Exposition*, p. 321.
18 Rogers, "report," p. 1.
19 Buel, *Fair*, vol. 8, p. v. Although Russia had originally planned an extensive educational exhibit, her entrance into the war with Japan in February 1904 resulted in the cancellation of the display.
20 "Minutes of Conference by the Directors of the Louisiana Purchase Exposition," October 22, 1902. Louisiana Purchase Exposition Manuscript Collection, Missouri Historical Society, St. Louis, Missouri.
21 Rogers, "Education Exhibit," p. 7.
22 Edmund Philbert mss, Philbert Papers, September 28, 1904. Philbert's journal is included in the manuscript collection of the Missouri Historical Society, St. Louis, Missouri.
23 *Report of the Board of Education, St. Louis, 1903-1904*, pp. 147-157.
24 *Ibid.*
25 *Ibid.* A brief detailed outline of the materials exhibited and the classes held by the school system in conjunction with the Exposition is included in *Brief Description of the World's Fair Exhibit* (St. Louis: St. Louis School Board, 1904).
26 For background on the founding and development of the Educational Museum of the St. Louis Public Schools see: Eugene F. Provenzo, Jr., "The Educational Museum of the St. Louis Public Schools," *The Bulletin* (Missouri Historical Society), Vol. 35, no. 3, April 1979, pp. 147-153.
27 *Public School Messenger* (St. Louis Public Schools), 13, no. 8, December 13, 1904, p. 800.
28 Elizabeth Golterman, "The Programs of Audio-Visual Education in City School Systems," *Forty-Eighth Yearbook of the National Society for the Study of Education* (Chicago: University of Chicago Press, 1949), p. 128.

29　F. Dean McCluskey, "A.-V. 1905-1955," *Educational Screen*, April 1955, pp. 160-162.

30　Oral History Interview of Amelia Meissner by Elizabeth Golterman and Charles Gilbert, October 2, 1952 at Pevely, Missouri. This interview is included in the historical file of the St. Louis Public Schools.

31　C. G. Rathman, "Report of the First Year's Work of the Educational Museum, 1905-1906," p. 1. This manuscript is included in the historical file of the St. Louis Public Schools.

32　*Public School Messenger* (St. Louis Public Schools), 45, September 12, 1905, p. 92.

33　John Philbrick, "Technological Museums," United States Bureau of Education, *Circulares of Information for 1880*, p. 60.

34　S. M. Green, "What Teachers May Learn From the Model School for the Deaf and Blind, And Their Exhibits," *N.E.A. Proceedings*, St. Louis (1904), pp. 937-939.

35　Mary R. Campbell, "The Chicago Hospital School for Nervous and Delicate Children—Its Educational and Scientific Methods," *N.E.A. Proceedings*, St. Louis (1904), pp. 962.

36　Buel, *Fair*, vol. 8, p. 2898.

37　Keller's visit to the Louisiana Purchase Exposition was widely covered in the Press, as well as in popular sources such as the children's magazine *St. Nicholas*.

38　*Ibid.* See the illustration and caption for "The Blind Twins from Kansas," included between pages 2998 and 2999.

39　"Report of the Representative of the Smithsonian Institution and National Museum, Louisiana Purchase Exposition, St. Louis, Mo., 1904, Appendix VIII," *Annual Report of the Board of Regents of the Smithsonian Institution... for the Year Ending June 30, 1904* (Washington, DC: Government Printing Office, 1905), p. 100.

40　*Ibid.*

41　*Ibid.*, p. 101.

42　Footnote from Smithsonian Reports, etc.

43　*Ibid.*

44　*Ibid.*, p. 102.

45　*Ibid.*, pp. 102-103.

46　Frederic W. Lehmann to D. R. Francis, August 31, 1901, in Library of Congress, Manuscripts Division, W. J. McGee Papers, box 3, folder F.

47　Robert W. Rydell, *All the World's a Fair: Vision of Empire at American International Expositions, 1876-1916* (Chicago: The University of Chicago Press, 1984), pp. 100, 160.

48　My interpretation and background for this section is drawn directly from Rydell. Those reader interested in a more detailed examination of McGee and his work during this period should refer to pp. 160-167 of Rydell, *All the World's a Fair*.

49 Ibid., p. 160.
50 Ibid., p. 161.
51 Quoted by Rydell, *All the World's a Fair*, p. 162.
52 Ibid.
53 Ibid.
54 Ibid., pp. 163 and 167.
55 Ibid., p. 168.
56 Quoted by Rydell, *All the World's a Fair*, p. 167.
57 Ibid., pp. 170-171.
58 Ibid., p. 170.
59 Ibid., p. 171.
60 Ibid., pp. 176-177.
61 Buel, *Fair*, p. 3761.
62 Rydell, *All the World's a Fair*, p. 178.
63 Ibid., p. 3755.
64 A. R. Hager, "The Educational Exhibit," *Report of the Philippine Exposition Board in the United States for the Louisiana Purchase Exposition* (Washington, DC: Bureau of Insular Affairs, War Department, 1905), p. 13.
65 Ibid., p. 14.
66 Ibid.
67 E. B. Bryan, "Education in the Philippines," NEA Proceedings, p. 103.
68 For background on Conial models of Education See: Philip J. Altbach and Gail Paradise Kelly, *Education and Colonialism* (New York: Longman, 1978).
69 Maria Del Pilar Zamora, "A Filipino's View of Education in the Philippines," NEA Proceedings, p. 471.
70 Rydell, *All the World's a Fair*, p. 183.
71 Russell M. Magnaghi, "America Views Her Indians at the 1904 World's Fair in St. Louis," *Gateway Heritage*, 4, no. 3, Winter 1983-1984, pp. 21-22.
72 Quoted by Magnaghi, op. cit., p. 24.
73 Ibid., p. 24.
74 Ibid.
75 Ibid.
76 Ibid., p. 25 and 27.
77 Ibid., p. 27.
78 A. M. Dockery, "Addresses of Welcome," *National Education Association Proceedings* (1904), p. 965.

79 Calvin Woodward, "Addresses of Welcome," *National Education Association Proceedings* (1904), p. 968.
80 Howard J. Rogers, "Foreign Educational Exhibits at the St. Louis Exposition," Louisiana Purchase Exposition Manuscript Collection, Missouri Historical Society, St. Louis, Missouri.
81 *Ibid.*, p. 4.
82 *Ibid.*, pp. 5-6.
83 Francis, *Universal Exposition*, p. 329.
84 Edward V. P. Schneiderhahn ms. diaries, vol. 6 (of 7 vols.), p. 83. Schneiderhahn's diary is included in the manuscript collection of the Missouri Historical Society, St. Louis, Missouri.
85 Rogers, "Report," p. 7.
86 *Ibid.*, p. 10.
87 Howard J. Rogers, "Department of International Congresses... Report of the Director," pp. 61-63. Louisiana Purchase Manuscript Collection, Missouri Historical Society, St. Louis, Missouri.
88 David Francis, "Addresses of Welcome," *National Educational Association, Journal of Proceedings and Addresses of the Forty-Third Annual Meeting Held at St. Louis Missouri in Connection with the Louisiana Purchase Exposition, June 27-July 1, 1904* (Winona, MN: National Educational Association, 1904), p. 50.
89 *Ibid.*, p. 51.
90 *Ibid.*, p. 52.
91 William T. Harris, "Addresses of Welcome," *National Educational Association, Journal of Proceedings and Addresses of the Forty-Third Annual Meeting Held at St. Louis Missouri in Connection with the Louisiana Purchase Exposition, June 27-July 1, 1904* (Winona, MN: National Educational Association, 1904), p. 56.
92 *Ibid.*, p. 57.
93 Rogers, "Department of International Congress... Report of the Director," p. 59.
94 Francis, *Universal Exposition*, p. 614.
95 Francis, "Addresses of Welcome," pp. 54-55.
96 *N.E.A. Proceedings* (1904), p. 114.

Conclusion
Culture as Curriculum

Cover of *Frank Leslie's Illustrated Historical Register of The Centennial Exposition 1876* (New York: Frank Leslie's, 1877).

The 1904 Louisiana Purchase Exposition in St. Louis was the last of the great international expositions. As David R. Francis, president of the Fair so clearly sensed, it would "be about the last exposition of this universal character that will be held during this generation..."[1] Although American expositions were subsequently held in Portland (1905), Seattle (1907), San Francisco (1915) and San Diego (1915-1916), it was at the St. Louis fair that the exposition movement reached its apex, both here and abroad.[2]

St. Louis was also the fair that finally placed education first and foremost in its scheme of classification and organization. As W. S. Chaplin, the chancellor of Washington University explained at the ceremonies opening the Louisiana Purchase Exposition:

> ...this Exhibition...is the first one that has ever given the highest prominence to the subject of education. It is a mark of the intelligence of the governing body of this Exposition that its chief department, the one to which it has given the most prominent place and on which it has expended the largest amount of money, is the Department of Education.[3]

In reading the Addresses of Welcome given for the opening ceremonies of the Louisiana Purchase Exposition, there can be found beneath the rhetoric, a coherent philosophy concerning the racial superiority the American people (and to some extent European), and more specifically of White-Anglo Saxon culture. David Francis at the opening of the Fair proclaimed, for example that:

> ...this universal exposition is more than an exhibition of products or even of processes: it is more than a congregating of the grades of civilization, as represented by all races from the primitive to the cultured: it is even more than a symposium of the thought of the thrones of the student and the moralist. It is all of these combined, and the tout ensemble forms a distinct entity whose impress on the present and influence on the future are deep and lasting.[4]

For Frederick J. Skiff, religious imagery came to mind reflecting an almost utopian or millenarian vision.

> The scene which stretches before us today is fairer than that upon which Christians gazed from the Delectable Mountain.... A person must be exalted at such a moment as this; the inauguration of the greatest educational force that has ever made its impress on humanity...[5]

For him, the Louisiana Purchase Exposition and the international expositions in general represented "a vast museum in motion."[6]

Quotes such as these echo sentiments that were repeated not only throughout the fair in St. Louis, but at the expositions held in Philadelphia in 1876 and Chicago in 1893. They are indicative of the role which the organizers and supporters of the expositions felt that the exhibits should play in the shaping the culture in which they lived. They point to the fact that the expositions, and the educational exhibits that were included in them, had as much to do with questions related to power and hegemony as learning and enlightenment. Ultimately, it is in the context of the relationship between power and knowledge that the expositions must be understood.

Significantly, the equation of knowledge and power was one that was understood by many of those who visited or participated in the exhibits and displays at the exposition. Henry Adams, in his various comments about the expositions in Philadelphia, Chicago, Paris and St. Louis, was clearly aware of their significance in this context. Perhaps no one, however, addressed the issue as clearly as J. George Hodgins, the Ontario commissioner of education for the 1876 Philadelphia Centennial Exhibition, when he declared that the international expositions were demonstrations of the maxim that:

> ..."knowledge is indeed power"—power which is irresistible—power, which with unerring penetration and force, seizes upon salient points; and, by controlling, turns even opposing forces into obedient servants of a superior will and design.[7]

In the United States, the "superior will and design" alluded to by Hodgins was that of a business-oriented, white, Anglo-Saxon, Protestant culture. As Robert Rydell has explained, besides promoting regional, national and international economic interests, the:

> ...exposition promoters also saw the fairs as vehicles for maintaining, or raising, their own status as regional or national leaders and for winning broad acceptance across class lines for *their* priorities and *their* decision-making authority.[8]

The expositions and their educational exhibits confirmed the power and the dominance of its organizers. It taught the superiority of Western ideas and Western education.

The educational exhibits at Philadelphia, Chicago and St. Louis were clearly part of a larger discourse on Western and modern capitalistic culture—what the French social historian Michel Foucault refers to as a "discursive field."[9] While the individual educational exhibits stood by themselves, they combined together to create a larger discourse and representation of culture and education—one which represented a selective construction of social reality, one which was also often highly self-serving, and perpetuated existing cultural and hegemonic systems.

In this context, I am drawn in my interpretation to the work of the comparative literary theorist Edward Said. In *Orientalism*, Said argues that Arab culture (North Africa, the Middle East, India, etc.) has been specifically constructed by Western writers and intellectuals through a process of "Orientalism" in a way that not only distorts the realities of Arab life, but which allows the West to dominate it. As Said explains, taking the eighteenth century as a starting point: "…Orientalism can be discussed and analyzed as the corporate institution for dealing with the Orient—dealing with it by making statements about it, authorizing views of it, describing it, by teaching it, settling it, ruling over it."[10]

Said recognizes that Orientalism is a discourse of the type described by Foucault.[11] For Said, Orientalism is not simply a structure of "lies and myths" about the Orient. Instead he argues:

> …Orientalism is more particularly valuable as a sign of European-Atlantic power over the Orient more than it is a veridic discourse about the Orient (which is what, in its academic or scholarly form, it claims to be).[12]

I believe that in much the same way that Orientalism is "a sign of European-Atlantic power" for the Arab world, that the construction of "knowledge and power" articulated by Hodgins in the context of education and international expositions, was part of the same, or at least, a closely related phenomenon.

It is clear that in the end, the expositions were not simply charming late Victorian diversions and entertainments. Instead, they were manifestations of hegemonic forces at work within the culture. In the more specific case of the educational exhibits, along with the demonstration and dissemination of important educational innovations, was also the empowerment of a new educational elite and a philosophy that promoted the superiority of the American people and their educational system. In conclusion, it is ultimately in this context that the expositions and their educational exhibits must be understood. As such, they represent a significant force in the history of American culture and education, and need to be understand not just as charming historical diversions, but as tools in the construction of a Western and American cultural vision that is more closely connected to themes of Imperialism and cultural domination than may at first seem to be the case.

Finally, the educational exhibits at the expositions need to be understood as critical transfer points for the exchange of educational ideas and innovations between Europe and the United States, as well as Asia. While the rhetoric of the schools as a democratic force for progress (as well as cultural domination) is clearly emphasized in the organization and descriptions of the American, and to a lesser degree, the European exhibits, it also needs to be remembered how much their content provided the basis for innovations in schooling not only in the United States, but also overseas. Thus in 1876, Americans were introduced to models of Russian manual training, and in 1893 to Swedish models of manual instruction, that probably would not have otherwise occurred. In the reverse direction, the Japanese in 1876 were provided European and American models of Kindergarten education, as well as new ideas about library organization and classification, and so on.

In the educational exhibits at the International Expositions, we see some of the earliest manifestations of the field of comparative education. The exhibits were conveyors of innovative curriculums—i.e., the content of instruction—to the world at large. In doing so, it can be argued that there is evidence in the expositions and their educational exhibits of the beginnings of a system of universal instruction—a global model for education—whose importance to modernization and globalism, as well as to cultural domination and hegemony needs to be understood in more detail.

In conclusion, the expositions and their educational exhibits represented cultural forces that are far more important than has been realized up until this time in shaping modern education. In doing so, they were not only forces for innovation and change, but also unique models of cultural domination and control. As such, they deserve significantly greater attention than has been assigned to them by historians of education in defining the shape and purpose of American, European and global education.

Notes

1 David Francis, "Addresses of Welcome," *National Educational Association, Journal of Proceedings and Addresses of the Forty-Third Annual Meeting Held at St. Louis Missouri in Connection with the Louisiana Purchase Exposition, June 27–July 1, 1904* (Winona, MN: National Educational Association, 1904), p. 51.

2 In terms of education and the expositions held after the 1904 fair in St. Louis, only the Panama-Pacific International Exposition held in San Francisco in 1915 has any sort of significant content related to education. The fair in San Francisco is of interest for a number reasons including the first public demonstration in the United States by Maria Montessori of her work. Of particular interest in light of racial theories put forward at previous expositions were the discussions as part of

the Education Conference concerning the use of Intelligence Quotient (IQ) exams and related issues of eugenics and race betterment. Concerning this topic see Rydell, pp. 223-225.

3   W. S. Chaplin, "Addresses of Welcome," *National Educational Association, Journal of Proceedings and Addresses of the Forty-Third Annual Meeting Held at St. Louis Missouri in Connection with the Louisiana Purchase Exposition, June 27-July 1, 1904* (Winona, Minn.: National Educational Association, 1904), p. 54.

4   "President Francis Tells the History of the Fair," *St. Louis Post Dispatch*, May 1, 1904, p. 4a. The secretary of war, William H. Taft, sent by President Theodore Roosevelt as his representative for the opening of the fair, reflected similar sentiments when he declared that the exposition represented:

> ...a great milestone in the united progress of the world. Each nation is here striving to show how, since the last great world's exposition, it has handled and added to the talent confided to its care. This is the union of nation toward higher material and spiritual existence. It is the measuring rod of that for which myriads of hands and myriads of brains have been striving—an increase in the control which mind and muscle have over the inanimate resources that nature furnishes... It reduces the size of our world in that it brings all the nations into one small locality for a time, but it increases enormously the efficiency engaged in carrying on the world's progress, by enabling each to gather the benefit of the other's work.

See: "Short Cut to Freedom For Filipinos, Says Sec'y Taft," *St. Louis Post Dispatch*, May 1, 1904, p. 4a.

5   "Exhibit Chief Advises Study of the Fair For Permanent Benefit," *St. Louis Post Dispatch*, May 1, 1904, p. 10a.

6   Ibid.

7   J. George Hodgins, *Special Report to the Honorable The Minister of Education, On the Ontario Educational Exhibit, And the Educational Features of the International Exhibition, At Philadelphia, 1876* (Toronto: Hunter, Rose & Co., 1877), pp. 231-232.

8   Robert Rydell, *All the World's a Fair: Visions of Empire at American International Expositions, 1876-1916* (Chicago: University of Chicago Press, 1984), p. 235.

9   Ibid., p. 245. According to Foucault:

> To say that statements are residual (remanent) is not to say that they remain in the field of memory, or that it is possible to rediscover what they meant; but it means that they are preserved by virtue of a number of supports and material techniques (of which the book is, of course, only one example), in accordance with certain types of institutions (of which the library is one), and with certain statutory modalities (which are not the same in the case of a religious text, a law, or a scientific truth). This also means that they are invested in techniques that put them into operation, in practices that derive from

them, in the social relations that they form, or, through those relations, modify.

See: Michel Foucault, *The Archaeology of Knowledge & The Discourse on Language* (New York: Harper, 1972), p. 245.

10 Edward W. Said, *Orientalism* (New York: Vintage Books, 1978), p. 3.
11 *Ibid.*, p. 3.
12 *Ibid.*, p. 6.

Bibliography

I. Archives, Libraries and Museums Consulted

Bancroft Library, University of California, Berkeley

Beinecke Library, Yale University

Buffalo and Erie County Historical Society

Chicago Historical Society

City Archives of Philadelphia

Free Library of Philadelphia

Historical Society of Pennsylvania

Library of Congress

Olin Library, Washington University

Missouri Historical Society

National Archives

National Museum of American History, Smithsonian Institution

Newberry Library, Chicago

New York Public Library

John Olin Library, Washington University

Otto G. Richter Library, University of Miami

Regenstein Library, University of Chicago

St. Louis Public Library

St. Louis Public Schools Archives

Smithsonian Institution Archives

Sterling Library, Yale University

Teachers College Library, Columbia University

II. Guidebooks, Pamphlets, Broadsides and Other Primary Sources

Adams, Henry. *The Education of Henry Adams.* New York: The Modern Library, 1931. Originally published 1907.

American Association of School Administrators. *Schedule for the Preparation of Students' Work for the Centennial Exhibition.* Washington, DC: Government Printing Office, 1875.

American Education as Described by the French Commission to the International Exhibition of 1876, Bureau of Education. Circular of Information No. 5 (1879). Bureau of Education. Washington, DC: Government Printing Office, 1879.

An Outline History of Japanese Education. New York: D. Appleton and Co., 1876.

Annual Report of the Board of Education of the State of Connecticut, presented to the General Assembly, January Session, 1877, Together with the Annual Report of the Secretary of the Board. New Haven, CT: Tuttle, Morehouse & Taylor, 1877.

Annual Report, United States Commissioner of Education. Washington, DC: United States Government Printing Office, 1874.

Atkin, Percy. "Popular Education in England." *Addresses and Proceedings of the National Educational Association.* St. Louis (1904):83-88.

Bancroft, Hubert Howe. *The Book of the Fair.* 2 Vols. Chicago: The Bancroft Co., 1895.

Bates, Clara Doty. "The Children's Building of the Columbian Exposition." *St. Nicholas,* 20, No. 9 (July, 1893):714-715.

Brief Description of the World's Fair Exhibit. St. Louis: St. Louis School Board, 1904.

Bryan, E. B. "Education in the Philippines." *Addresses and Proceedings of the National Educational Association.* St. Louis (1904):100-104.

Buel, J. W., ed. *Louisiana and the Fair: An Exposition of the World, Its People, and Their Achievements.* 10 vols. St. Louis: World's Progress Publishing Company, 1905.

Buisson, M. Ferdinand, et al. *Rapport sur l'instruction primaire a l'exposition universelle de Philadelphie en 1876.* Paris: Imprimerie nationale, 1878.

Butler, Nicholas Murray, ed. *Monographs on Education in the United States.* 2 vols. Albany, NY: J. B. Lyons Co., 1900.

Campbell, Mary R. "The Chicago Hospital School for Nervous and Delicate Children—Its Educational and Scientific Methods." *Addresses and Proceedings of the National Educational Association.* St. Louis (1904):952-962.

Cantley, A. C. "Education Stands First at the World's Fair," *Kindergarten Magazine,* 16, no. 10 (June 1904):403-409.

Bibliography

Carr, Mrs. Jeanne C. "Educational Progress, As Exemplified at the Centennial Exhibition." *Seventh Biennial Report of the Superintendent of Public Instruction of the State of California for the School Years 1876 and 1877.* Sacramento, CA: State Printing Office, 1877: 30-45.

Catalogue of the Collective Exposition at the Centennial Exhibition in 1876 at Philadelphia, of the Netherlands Booksellers' Association. Amsterdam, 1876.

Catalog of Connecticut Educational Exhibit. No Imprint. 1893.

Catalogue of the Manual Training School of Washington University, 1913-1914. St. Louis, MO, 1914.

Catalogue of the Russian Section, International Exhibition of 1876. C. HETEPBYPTb, 1876.

"Catholic Education at the World's Fair." *The Catholic World,* 58 (1893-4):186-203.

"The Catholic Educational Exhibit in the Columbian Exposition." *The Catholic World,* 55 (1892):580-587.

The Catholic Educational Exhibit at the World's Fair Columbian Exposition. Chicago: J. S. Hyland, 1896.

"The Catholic School Exhibit." *The Catholic World* (July, 1894):538-554.

"The Centennial Aspect of the Exposition" *New-England Journal of Education,* 3, no. 23 (June 3, 1876):271.

Centennial Exposition Guide. Philadelphia: G. Lawrence, [1876?].

"Characteristics of the International Fair." *The Atlantic Monthly,* October, 1876:492-495.

"Children's Building." *World's Columbian Exposition Illustrated,* 3, no. 5 (July, 1893): 122.

Clarke, I. Edwards. *Industrial and High Art Education in the United States. Part I. Drawing in Public Schools.* Washington, DC: Government Printing Office, 1885.

Clarke, Isaac Edwards. *Art and Industry. Education in the Industrial and Fine Arts in the United States.* Washington, DC: Government Printing Office, 1892.

"Columbian Bulletin, American Business Colleges." Manufactures Building, Exposition Grounds, Chicago, July, 1893.

"Columbian Catholic Congress at Chicago." *The Catholic World,* 57 (1893):604-608.

Columbian History of Education in Kansas. Topeka, KS: Press of the Hamilton Printing Company, 1893.

Compayre, Gabriel. "The Congresses of Education of Chicago." *Education*, 14 (April, 1894):487-496; (May, 1894):552-558.

Compayre, Gabriel. "A Foreigner's Impressions of the Chicago Educational Congresses." *Educational Review*, 6 (October, 1893):257-267.

"Connecticut Schools Document." *Catalogue of Connecticut Educational Exhibit*. No. 9 (1893). No Imprint.

Della Vos, Victor. *Description of the Collections of Scientific Appliances Instituted for the Study of Mechanical Art in Workshops of the Imperial Technical School of Moscow*. Moscow, 1876.

Eaton, John. "The Exhibit of Education at the Columbian Exposition." *Addresses and Proceedings of the National Educational Association*. Asbury Park, NJ, 1894: 515-527.

Eaton, John. "The Exhibit of Education at the Columbian Exposition." *Report of the Commissioner of Education for the Year 1892-93*. 1:445-454. Washington, DC: Government Printing Office, 1895.

Eaton, John. *Notes on Education at the Columbian Exposition*. Washington, DC: Government Printing Office, 1896.

Editorials. *The Library Journal*, September 30, 1876: 12-15; November 30, 1876: 90-93, 113, 118-121, 140-145.

"The Educational Exhibit of Foreign Countries." *Weekly State Gazette*, July 27, 1876.

1876: A Centennial Offering by Third Ward Pupils. No. 10, Des Moines, Iowa. Reprint. Ames, IA: The Iowa State University Press, 1977.

The Empire of Brazil at the Universal Exhibition of 1876 in Philadelphia. Rio De Janeiro: Typographia e Lithographia do Imperial Instituto Artistico, 1876.

"Exhibit of Russian Educational and Charitable Institutions." *World's Columbian Exposition Illustrated*, 3, no. 5 (July, 1893): 128.

"Exhibits of Foreign Technical Schools at the Centennial." *Scientific American*, 35, no. 8 (August 19, 1876): 120.

Exhibits of the State of New York at the World's Columbian Exposition. Chicago, 1893.

Final Report of the Ohio State Board of Centennial Managers to the General Assembly of the State of Ohio. Columbus, OH: Nevins & Myers, State Printers, 1877.

Fortieth Annual Report of the Superintendent of Public Instruction of the State of Michigan, with Accompanying Documents, for the Year 1876. Lansing, MI: W. S. George & Co., n.d.

Foy, Peter L. "The Forthcoming Catholic Congress." *American Catholic Quarterly Review*, 14 (1889):542-551.

Francis, David R. *The Universal Exposition of 1904*. St. Louis: Louisiana Purchase Exposition Company, 1913.

Goode, George Brown. "First Draft of a System of Classification for the World's Columbian Exposition." *Report of the U. S. National Museum under the Direction of the Smithsonian Institution for the Year Ending June 30, 1891*. Washington, DC, 1891.

The Great Exhibition, London (Facsimile of the 1851 *Art Journal Illustrated Catalogue of the Industries of All Nations*). New York: Crown Books, 1970.

The Greatest of Expositions. Completely Illustrated. St. Louis, MO: The Official Photographic Company of the Louisiana Purchase Exposition, 1904.

Green, S. M. "What Teachers May Learn From the Model School for the Deaf and Blind, And Their Exhibits." *Addresses and Proceedings of the National Educational Association*. St. Louis (1904): 937–939.

Hager, A. R. "The Educational Exhibit." *Report of the Philippine Exposition Board in the United States for the Louisiana Purchase Exposition*. Washington, DC: Bureau of Insular Affairs, War Department, 1905.

Harrington, H. F. "The Educational Exhibit at Philadelphia" *New England Journal of Education*, 4, no. 98 (Dec. 16, 1876): 267.

Harris, William Torrey. "Census of 1880." *American Journal of Education*. n.d.:6. Manuscript Division, Library of Congress.

Harris, William Torrey. "The Centennial Exposition." *Twenty-Second Annual Report of the Board of Directors of the St. Louis Public Schools for the Year Ending August 1, 1876*. St. Louis: Slawson, Printer, 1877.

Harris, William Torrey. "The Educational Significance of the Centennial Exposition." *Address, State Teachers' Convention, Springfield, Mass.*, December 1876. Manuscript Division, Library of Congress.

Harris, William Torrey. "The Work of the Educational Congress." *The Independent*, 45 (August 3, 1893): 1034.

Harris, William Torrey. "The World's Educational Congress." Address before the National Educational Association, Department of Superintendents, 1892. Manuscripts. Library of Congress.

Hausknect, Emil. "The American System of Education." *Report of the American Commissioner of Education, 1892–93*. No Imprint. 521–533.

Heller, Otto. "The Improvement of Education." *The World's Work*. Special Double Exposition Number (August 1904):5115–5122.

Hodgins, J. George. *Special Report to the Honorable The Minister of Education, On the Ontario Educational Exhibit, And the Educational Features of the International Exhibition, At Philadelphia, 1876.* Toronto, ON: Hunter, Rose & Co., 1877.

Howells, William Dean. *Letters of an Altrurian Traveller.* Edited by Clara M. Kirk and Rudolph King. Gainesville, FL: Scholar's Facsimiles & Reprints, 1961.

"The Indian Education Exhibit, Centennial Exposition." *New England Journal of Education,* 4, no. 10 (September 16, 1876): 115.

Ingram, J. S. *The Centennial Exposition.* Philadelphia: Hubbard Bros., 1876.

The International Conference on Education held at Philadelphia, July 17 and 18, in connection with the International Exhibition of 1876. Department of the Interior, Bureau of Education. Washington, DC: Government Printing Office, 1877.

International Exhibition. Department of Education and Science. Catalogue of some of the Prominent Exhibits in this Department from Massachusetts. Philadelphia: A. C. Bryson & Co., 1876.

International Exhibition 1876. Connecticut in the Department of Education and Science at Philadelphia. New Haven, CT: B. G. Northrup, December 20, 1875.

International Exhibition 1876. Department of Education and Science. Catalogue of the New Jersey Exhibit. Trenton, NJ: Noar, Day and Noar, 1876.

International Exhibition 1876. Reports and Awards Group XXVIII. Edited by Francis A. Walker. Philadelphia: Lippincott & Co., 1878.

International Exhibition 1876 at Philadelphia. Portuguese Special Catalogue. Departments I., II., III., IV., V.: Mining and Metallurgy, Manufactures, Education and Science, Fine Arts, Machinery. No Imprint.

Johnson, Rossiter, ed. *A History of the World's Columbian Exposition Held in Chicago in 1893.* 4 vols. New York: D. Appleton and Company, 1898.

Kasson, Frank H. "Chicago and the Congress of Education." *Education.* XIV (September, 1893):32–36.

Kasson, Frank H. "Glimpses of the Fair." *Education,* 14 (October, 1893): 104–108.

Larson, Gustaf. "Sloyd for Elementary Schools Contrasted with the Russian System of Manual Training." *Proceedings of the National Education Association* (International Congress of Education), 32 (1893): 600–601.

"Letters About the Exhibition." *New York Tribune,* extra no. 35:n.d. [1876]

Lowenstein, M. J. *Official Guide to the Louisiana Purchase Exposition.* Saint Louis: Official Guide Company, 1904.

McCabe, James D. *The Illustrated History of the Centennial Exhibition*. Philadelphia: National Publishing Co., 1876.

Metric-Diagram of Fairmont Park, Machinery Hall, The Women's Pavilion, and the Agricultural Building, Philadelphia Centennial Exhibition, 1876. Hartford, CT: The Case, Lockwood and Brainard Co., n. d. [1876].

"Meeting of the Executive Committee of the United States Centennial Commission, Philadelphia, August, 1872." From *The Philadelphia Inquirer*, August 28, 30, 1872.

Meissner, Amelia. Oral History Interview by Elizabeth Golterman and Charles Gilbert, October 2, 1952 at Pevely, Missouri. St. Louis Public Schools Archives.

Ministere de l'education Nationale. *American Education as Described by the French Commission to the International Exhibition of 1876*. Washington, DC: Government Printing Office, 1879.

"Minutes of Conference by the Directors of the Louisiana Purchase Exposition." October 22, 1902. Missouri Historical Society.

Muldoon, P. J., ed. *The World's Columbian Catholic Congresses and Educational Exhibit*. Chicago: J. S. Hyland & Company, 1893.

National Education Association of the United States. *Proceedings of the International Congress of Education of the World's Columbian Exposition, Chicago, July 25–28, 1893*. New York: National Education Association, 1895.

Northrop, Birdsey Grant. *Lessons from European Schools and the American Centennial*. New York: A. S. Barnes & Co., 1877.

Norwegian Special Catalogue for the International Exhibition at Philadelphia, 1876. Christiania: Printed by B. M. Bentzen, 1876.

"Notes Concerning the Department of Education at the Universal Exposition, St. Louis, 1904." *Kindergarten Magazine*, 16, no. 10 (June 1904): 397–402.

Official Catalogue of Exhibits: Section II. Saint Louis: Official Catalogue Company, 1904.

Official Catalogue of Exhibits, Universal Exposition, St. Louis, 1904. St. Louis: Official Catalogue Company, [1904].

Official Handbook of the Philippines and Catalogue of the Philippine Exhibit. Manila: Bureau of Public Printing, 1903.

Ohio. *Historical Sketches of Public Schools in Cities, Villages and Townships in the State of Ohio*. n.p., 1876.

Ohio. *Historical Sketches of the Higher Educational Institutions*. n.p., 1876.

"Opening of the International Exhibition." *Scientific American Supplement*, no. 22 (May 27, 1876):338–339.

Peabody, Elizabeth. *Kindergarten Messenger* [New England Journal of Education], 6 (June 10, 1876):285.

Peabody, Selim H. "The Educational Exhibit at the Columbian Exposition." *Addresses and Proceedings of the National Educational Association.* Asbury Park, NJ, 1894: 60-66.

Peabody, Selim H. *The Educational Exhibit of the World's Columbian Exhibit.* World's Columbian Exposition Department of Liberal Arts, Circular No. 2. [1893]

Peabody, Selim. H. *Educational Exhibit of the World's Columbian Exposition.* No. 3., n.p., 1893.

Pennsylvania at the Centennial Exhibition of 1876. Harrisburg, PA: B. F. Meyers, 1875.

Philadelphia International Exhibition, 1876. Mexican Section. Special Catalogue and Explanatory Notes. Philadelphia: Dan. F. Gillin, Printer, 1876.

Philadelphia International Exhibition, 1876. Official Catalogue of the British Section. Part I. London: Printed by George E. Eyre and William Spottiswoode, 1876.

Philbert, Edmund. Manuscript. September 28, 1904. Missouri Historical Society.

Philbrick, John. "Technological Museums." *Circulars of Information for 1880.* United States Bureau of Education, 60.

"Prospects of the Department of Education." *Scientific American Supplement,* no. 6 (February 5, 1876):82.

Public School Messenger. St. Louis Public Schools, 1904, 1905.

Rathman, C. G. "Report of the First Year's Work of the Educational Museum, 1905-1906." Manuscript. St. Louis Public Schools Archives.

Report of the Board of Education. St. Louis: 1903-1904.

Report of the Board of General Managers of the Exhibit of the State of New York at the World's Columbian Exposition. Albany, NY: James B. Lyon, State Printer, 1894.

Report of the Illinois Board of World's Fair Commissioners at the World's Columbian Exposition, May 1-October 30, 1893. No Imprint.

Report of the Iowa Columbian Commission. Chicago, A.D. 1893. Cedar Rapids, IA: Republican Printing Company, 1895.

Report of the Kansas Board of World's Fair Managers. Topeka, KS: Press of the Hamilton Printing Company, 1894.

"Report of the Representative of the Smithsonian Institution and National Museum, Louisiana Purchase Exposition, St. Louis, Mo., 1904, Appendix VIII." *Annual Report of the Board of Regents of the Smithsonian Institution...for the Year Ending June 30, 1904.* Washington, DC: Government Printing Office, 1905.

Report of the State Board of Centennial Managers for the International Exhibition of 1876. [Michigan] Lansing, MI: W. S. George & Co., 1877.

Report of the Superintendent of Public Instruction of the Commonwealth of Pennsylvania for the Year ending June 1, 1876. Harrisburg, PA: B. F. Meyers, 1876.

Rogers, Howard J. "Educational Exhibit." *The Universal Exposition of 1904.* St. Louis, 1904. This was a regular publication printed at the time of the Exposition and should not be confused with David R. Francis' history of the Fair published under the same title in 1913.

Rose, Joshua., "The Handiwork of Apprentices at the Centennial Exposition: The Exhibit of the Imperial Technical School, Moscow." *Scientific American Supplement*, no.46 (November 11, 1876):721–722.

Runkle, John. "The Russian System of Mechanical Art Education, as Applied in the Massachusetts Institute of Technology." *National Education Association of the United States. Addresses and Proceedings.* Louisville, 1877.

"The Russian System of Trade Education." *Scientific American*, 35, no. 17 (October 21, 1876):265.

"Ruth R. Burritt." *Woman's Words*, 4, no. 9 (January, 1881): 607–608.

Schneiderhahn, Edward V. P. Diaries. Missouri Historical Society.

Sidenbladh, Elis. *Swedish Catalogue. I. Statistics. International Exhibition, 1876.* Philadelphia: No Imprint.

Sixty-Second Annual Report of the Massachusetts Board of Education: Together with the Sixty-Second Annual Report of the Secretary of the Board, 1897–1898. Boston: Wright & Potter Printing Co., 1899.

"The Sloyd Department." *Children's Building of the World's Columbian Exposition.* 1893:10–11.

Smith, Frank Webster, "Education at American Expositions." *Education*, 24, no. 4 (December 1903): 222–231.

Smithsonian Institution. *Exhibits at the World's Columbian Exposition.* Annual Report of the Smithsonian. Washington, DC: 1894.

Snider, Denton J. "The Organization of the Fair." *World's Fair Studies*, no. 2. Chicago: Chicago Kindergarten College, n. d.

Souvenir Manual of the Minnesota Educational Exhibit for the World's Columbian Exposition at Chicago, 1893. Minneapolis: Moffett, Thurston & Plank Printing Co., [1893].

Stetson, C. B. "Drawing as an Element of Advanced Industrial Education." *New England Journal of Education*, 4, no. 12 (September 23, 1876): 135–136; 4, no. 13 (October 7, 1876): 144.

"Sweden at the Centennial." *Scientific American Supplement*, no. 18 (April 29, 1876): 282.

Swett, John. *History of the Public School System of California*. San Francisco: A. L. Bancroft and Company, 1876.

"Technical Education in the United States as Illustrated at the Centennial." *Scientific American*, 35, no. 5 (July 29, 1876): 67–68.

Trybom, J. H. "Sloyd as an Educational Subject." *Proceedings of the National Education Association*, 31 (1892): 456.

Twenty-first Annual Report of the Board of Directors of the St. Louis Public Schools for the Year Ending August 1, 1875. St. Louis: Globe-Democrat Job Printing Co., 1876.

Twenty-second Annual Report of the Board of Directors of the St. Louis Public Schools, for the Year Ending August 1, 1876. St. Louis: Slawson, 1877.

United States National Museum. *Annual Report* (1896–97) (A Memorial to George Brown Goode). Washington, DC: U.S. Government Printing Office, 1897.

"A Vast Educational Influence." *Journal of Education*, 60, no. 11 (September 15, 1904): 193.

Violle, Jules. "The Chicago Exposition and American Science." *Report of the American Commissioner of Education, 1892–93*, p. 595.

Waetzoldt, Stephen. "The Educational Exhibit in Chicago and the School System of the United States." *Report of the Commissioner of Education for the Year 1892–93*, I: 556. Washington, DC: Government Printing Office, 1895.

Waetzoldt, Stephen. "The School System of the United States." *Report of the Commissioner of Education for the Year 1892–93*, I: 559. Washington, DC: Government Printing Office, 1895.

Walker, John Brisben. "The Education of the World as Shown in the Exhibits of Many Peoples." The World's Fair, IV. *The Cosmopolitan* (September, 1904): 497–512.

Walker, Francis A., ed. *Reports and Awards Group XXVIII: International Exhibition, 1876*. Philadelphia: Lippincott, 1878.

Waterman, Richard Jr. "International Education Congresses of 1893." *Educational Review*, 6 (September 1893):158–166.

Waterman, Richard Jr. "Educational Exhibits at the Columbian Exposition (I), *Educational Review*, 6 (October 1893):274.

Waterman, Richard Jr., "Educational Exhibits at World's Fairs Since 1851 (I)." *Educational Review*, 5 (February 1893):120-129.

Waterman, Richard Jr. "Educational Exhibits at World's Fairs Since 1851 (II)." *Educational Review*, 5 (March 1893):219-231.

White, E. E. "The Relation of Education to Industry." *Circulars of Information of the Bureau of Education*, no.2 (1881): 40-48. Washington, DC: Government Printing Office, 1881.

White, E. E. "Technical Training in American Schools." *Circulars of Information of the Bureau of Education*, no. 2 (1881): 33-39. Washington, DC: Government Printing Office, 1881.

Whitford, W. C. *Historical Sketch of Education in Wisconsin*. Madison, WI.: Atwood & Culber, 1876.

Wilson, J. Ormond. "The National Museum." *Addresses and Proceedings of the National Educational Association*. Louisville, KY, 1877: 56-58.

Winkler, Bertha. "Ruth R. Burritt." *Woman's Words*, 4, no. 9 (January 1881).

Woodward, C. M. *The Manual Training School*. Boston: D. C. Heath & Co., 1887.

World's Columbian Exposition, Plan and Classification. Chicago: Chicago's World's Columbian, Department of Publicity and Promotion, n.d.

Wright, Frank Lloyd. *An Autobiography*. New York: Duell, Sloan and Pearce, 1943.

Zamora, Maria Del Pilar. "A Filipino's View of Education in the Philippines." *Addresses and Proceedings of the National Educational Association*. St. Louis (1904): 468-471.

Zolnay, George. "Architecture at the Exposition." *Addresses and Proceedings of the National Education Association*. St. Louis (1904): 167-172.

The Youth's Companion. *World's Fair Extra Number*. Boston: Perry Mason Co., 1893.

IV. Secondary Sources

Alexander, Edward P. *Museum Masters: Their Museums and Their Influence*. Nashville, TN: The American Association for State and Local History, 1983.

Apple, Michael W. *Education and Power*. Boston: Routledge & Kegan Paul, 1983.

Apple, Michael W., ed. *Cultural and Economic Reproduction in Education: Essays on Class, Ideology and the State*. London: Routledge, Kegan & Paul, 1982.

Apple, Michael W. *Ideology and Curriculum*. London: Routledge & Kegan Paul, 1979.

Apple, Michael W. and Lois Weis, eds. *Ideology and Practice in Schooling*. Philadelphia: Temple University Press, 1983.

Badger, Reid. *The Great American Fair: The World's Columbian Exposition and American Culture* (1979).

Bailyn, Bernard. *Education and the Forming of American Society*. New York: Norton, 1972.

Bennett, Charles. *History of Manual and Industrial Education 1870–1917*. Peoria, IL: The Manual Arts Press, 1937.

Braun, Judy Elise. *The North American Indian Exhibits at the 1876 and 1893 World Expositions: The Influence of Scientific Thought Upon Popular Attitudes*. Master's thesis, George Washington University, 1975.

Brown, Lee Alexander. *The Year of the Century*. New York: Scribner, 1966.

Burg, David F. *Chicago's White City of 1893* (1976).

Cawelti, John G. *Apostles of the Self-Made Man*. Chicago: University of Chicago Press, 1968.

Clarke, I. Edwards. *Industrial and High Art Education in the United States, Part I. Drawing in the Public Schools*. Washington, DC: Government Printing Office, 1885.

Coats, A. W. "American Scholarship Comes of Age: The Louisiana Purchase Exposition 1904." *Journal of the History of Ideas*, 22 (1961): 404–417.

Cortinovis, Irene E. "China at the St. Louis World's Fair." *Missouri Historical Review*. 72 (1977): 59–66.

Cremin, Lawrence. *American Education: The Colonial Experience, 1607–1783*. New York: Harper and Row, 1970.

Cremin, Lawrence. *American Education: The National Experience, 1783–1876*. New York: Harper and Row, 1980.

Cremin, Lawrence. *American Education: The Metropolitan Experience, 1876–1980*. New York: Harper and Row, 1988.

Cremin, Lawrence. *The Transformation of the School*. New York: Alfred A. Knopf, 1961.

Curti, Merle. "America at the World Fairs, 1851–1893." *American Historical Review*, 55(1950):833–56.

Darney, Virginia Grant. "Women and World's Fairs: American International Expositions, 1876–1904." Doctoral dissertation, Emory University, 1982.

Dye, Charles M. "Calvin Woodward and Manual Training: The Man, the Idea and the School." *The Bulletin* (Missouri Historical Society), 32, no. 3 (January 1976): 75–98.

The Early Writings of Frederick Jackson Turner, with a List of All His Works Compiled by Everett E. Edwards and an introduction by Fulmer Mood. Madison, WI: University of Wisconsin Press, 1938.

"Expositions, International and Education." *A Cyclopedia of Education.* edited by Paul Monroe. New York: The MacMillan Co., n.d.:555-558.

Fletcher, William I. *Public Libraries in America.* No. II. Boston: Roberts Brothers, 1894.

Foner, Philip S. "Black Participation in the Centennial of 1876." *Negro History Bulletin,* 39 (1976): 533-38.

Golterman, Elizabeth. "The Programs of Audio-Visual Education in City School Systems." *Forty-Eight Yearbook of the National Society for the Study of Education.* Chicago: University of Chicago Press, 1949.

Hoffman, Donald. *The Architecture of John Welborn Root.* Baltimore: Johns Hopkins University Press, 1973.

Hoxie, Frederick E. *A Final Promise: The Campaign to Assimilate the Indians, 1880-1920.* Lincoln: University of Nebraska Press, 1984.

Iriye, Akira, ed. *Mutual Images: Essays in American-Japanese Relations.* Cambridge, MA: Harvard University Press, 1975.

Korzenik, Diana. *Drawn to Art: A Nineteenth-Century American Dream.* Hanover: University Press of New England, 1985.

Maass, John. *The Glorious Enterprise. The Centennial Exhibition of 1876 and H. J. Schwarzmann, Architect-in-Chief.* Watkins Glen, NY: American Life Foundation, 1973.

Maass, John. "Who Invented Dewey's Classification?" *Wilson Library Bulletin,* 47 (Dec. 1972): 335-41.

Magnaghi, Russell M. "America Views Her Indians at the 1904 World's Fair in St. Louis." *Gateway Heritage,* 4, no.3 (Winter 1983-1984): 21-29.

Mason, Grant Carpenter. *Frank Lloyd Wright to 1910.* New York: Reinhold Publishing Corporation, 1958.

McCluskey, F. Dean. "A.-V. 1905-1955." *Educational Screen,* April 1955: 160-162.

Miner, Craig H. "The United States Government Building at the Centennial Exhibition, 1874-77." *Prologue. The Journal of the National Archives.* 4, no. 4 (Winter 1972):202-218.

Mumford, Louis. *The Brown Decades.* New York: Harcourt Brace and Co., 1931.

Post, Robert C. *1876: A Centennial Exhibition.* Washington, DC: The National Museum of History and Technology, 1976.

Pratt, Richard Henry. *Battlefield and Classroom: Four Decades with the American Indians, 1867-1904.* Edited with an introduction by Robert M. Utley. New Haven, CT: Yale University Press, 1964.

Provenzo, Eugene F., Jr. "Education and the Louisiana Purchase Exposition." *Missouri Historical Society Bulletin*, 32, no. 2 (January 1976): 99-109.

Provenzo, Eugene F., Jr. "The Educational Museum of the St. Louis Public Schools." *The Bulletin* (Missouri Historical Society), 35, no.3 (April 1979): 147-153.

Rosenberg, Emily S. *Spreading the American Dream. American Economic and Cultural Expansion, 1890-1945.* New York: Hill and Wang, 1982.

Ross, Elizabeth Dale. *The Kindergarten Crusade: The Establishment of Preschool Education in the United States.* Athens: Ohio University Press, 1976.

Rudwick, Elliott M., and August Meier. "Black Man in the 'White City': Negroes and the Columbian Exposition, 1893." *Phylon*, 26 (1965): 354-361.

Rydell, Robert W. *All the World's a Fair: Visions of Empire at American International Expositions, 1876-1916.* Chicago: University of Chicago Press, 1984.

Rydell, Robert W. "The World's Columbian Exposition of 1893: Racist Underpinnings of a Utopian Artifact." *Journal of American Culture*, 1 (1978): 253-275.

Sanders, James. *The Education of an Urban Minority*

Schuyler, Montgomery. "Last Words About the Fair." *American Architecture*, II. Cambridge, MA Harvard University Press, 1961.

Shapiro, Michael Steven. *Child's Garden: The Kindergarten Movement from Froebel to Dewey.* University Park: The Pennsylvania State University Press, 1983.

Smith, Henry Nash. *Virgin Land: The American West as Symbol and Myth.* Cambridge: Harvard University Press, 1950.

Sprague, Stuart Seely. "Meet Me In St. Louis on the Ten-Million-Dollar Pike." *The Bulletin* [Missouri Historical Society], 32 (1975): 26-31.

Stamp, Robert M. *The Schools of Ontario, 1876-1976.* Toronto, ON: University of Toronto Press, 1982.

Sullivan, Louis. *Kindergarten Chats and Other Writings.* New York: George Wittenborn, Inc., 1947.

Snyder, Agnes. *Dauntless Women in Childhood Education, 1856-1931.* Washington, DC: Association for Childhood Education International, 1972.

Trennert, Robert A. "Fairs, Expositions, and the Changing Image of Southwestern Indians, 1876-1904." *New Mexico Historical Review*, 62 (April, 1987): 127-150.

Vandewalker, Nina C. *The Kindergarten in American Education*. New York: Macmillan Co., 1908.

Weber, Evelyn. *The Kindergarten: Its Encounter with Educational Thought in America*. New York: Teachers College Press, 1969.

Weimann, Jeanne Madeline. *The Story of the Woman's Building, World's Columbian Exposition, Chicago 1893*. Chicago: Academy Chicago, 1981.

Williams, Raymond. "Base and Superstructure in Marxist Cultural Theory." *Schooling and Capitalism: A Sociological Reader*. London: Routledge & Kegan Paul, 1976: 204-205.

Winthrop, John. *Papers*. A. B. Forbes, ed. II: 295. Boston: Massachusetts Historical Society, 1931.

Winton, Ruth M. "Negro Participation in Southern Expositions, 1881-1915." *Journal of Negro Education*, 16 (Winter 1947): 34-43.

Woodward, Calvin M. *The Manual Training School*. Boston: D. C. Heath & Co., 1887.

Wylier, Irvin G. *The Self-Made Man in America*. New York: The Free Press, 1954.

INDEX

Adams, Charles Francis, 81
Adams, Henry, 3, 67, 68, 99, 132
Albert, Prince, 7
Angell, James B., 80
Apple, Michael, 6
Art education, at the Crystal Palace Exhibition, 28; realization for need of in the United States, 29-30;

Bailyn, Bernard, 6
Baird, Spencer Fullerton, 66
Bellamy, Francis J., 68
Bennett, Charles, 90
Blow, Susan, 35, 38
Bonney, Charles G. 91
Bradley, Milton, 35
Buisson, M. Ferdinand, 16, 17
Bureau of Indian Affairs' exhibit, at the World's Columbian Exposition, 78
Burritt, Ruth R., 36, 39

Carlisle Indian School, at the World's Columbian Exposition, 77
Catholic Educational exhibit, at the World's Columbian Exposition, 84-86
Centennial, the, as a school of patriotism, 16
Centennial History of American Education, 51-55
Children's Building, at the World's Columbian Exposition, 83
Chaplin, W. S., 131
Children's Room (Smithsonian Institution, at the Louisiana Purchase Exposition, Saint Louis), 109

Chinese, exhibits at the Philadelphia Centennial Exposition, 46
"City Upon a Hill", 72
Classification of exhibits, at the World's Columbian Exposition, 65, 67
Cliff dwellers exhibit, at the World's Columbian Exposition, 76
Colonialzation, American, 44-45
Corliss steam engine, 55
Craus-Boelte, Maria, 35
Cremin, Lawrence, 6, 52, 53
Crystal Palace Exposition (1851), 7; art education, at, 28
Cubberly, Ellwood P., 53-55; model for the history of American education, 53-55
Cygnaeus, Uno, 87

Decimal system of library classification, 41-44
"Defective" students (blind, deaf, dumb), model classes (Louisiana Purchase Exposition), 107-108
Della Vos, Victor, 23
Des Peres kindergarten (St. Louis), 35, 39
Dewey, Melvil, 41-43
Dockery, A. M., 118
Dwight, Timothy, 82
Dynamo, at the Paris 1900 Exposition, 2, 3

Eaton, John, 9, 16, 41, 71, 75, 83
Educational Congress, at the World's Columbian Exposition, 80

Ethnological displays, at the World's Columbian Exposition, 74-76

Field Museum (Chicago), 75
Francis, David R., 121-122, 123, 131
Frontier Thesis (Turner), 65
Froebel, Frederick, 36
Froebel's Gifts, 37-38
Foucault, Michel, 132-133

German Educational exhibit, at the World's Columbian Exposition, 82-83; at the Louisiana Purchase Exposition, 118, 119
Goode, G. Brown, 65, 67, 74

Hale, Edward Everett, 29
Hall, G. Stanley, 81
Harrington, H. F., 19
Harris, William Torrey, 18, 21, 29, 35, 41, 123
Harrison, H. F., 34
Hausknecht, Emil, 79
Hodgins, J. George, 3, 33
Hoxie, Frederick, 76
Hoyt, J. W., 8, 41

Illinois Industrial University, 22
Industrial education, 21
Industrialization, and enlightenment, 22
International Conference on Education, at the Philadelphia Centennial Exposition, 40-41
International Expositions (overview), 3-10; and cultural hegemony, 5, 6, 10; as a special creation of the second half of the nineteenth century, 7; as instruments of power, 4, 5

Japanese educational exhibit, at the Philadelphia Centennial Exposition, 46-47
Jorden, David Star, 81

Keller, Helen, 101
Kindergarten exhibits, at the Philadelphia Centennial Exposition, 34-39
"Knowledge is Power", 4, 10, 99, 124
Kovalesky, M. Ergraff, 81

Larsson, Gustaf, 88
Liberal Arts Building (World's Columbian Exposition), 70
Libraries, American, history of, 41
"Living ethnological" exhibits, at the Louisiana Purchase Exposition, 111-116
"Living" exhibits, at the World's Columbian Exposition, 75
Louisiana Purchase Exposition (Saint Louis, 1904), 97-128; "Defective" students (blind, deaf, dumb), model classes, 107-108; Education, as main theme, 100; German educational exhibits, 119; Geronimo, 118, 119; "Living ethnological exhibits, 111-116; Native American education exhibit, 116-118; Palace of Education, 102, 103, 104, 120; "Pike", 74; Philippine exhibit, 112-116, demonstration classes, 115; Saint Louis Public Schools exhibit, 104-106; Smithsonian Institution, 109, 110-112;
Low, Seth, 82

Manual Training School of Washington University (St. Louis), 28
Massachusetts Art Exhibit, at the Philadelphia Centennial Exposition, 31

Massachusetts Institute of Technology, 22
McCosh, James, 82
McDaniel, Frances, 36
McGee, W. J., 110-112
Mechanic Arts, Palace of, at the World's Columbian Exposition, 66
Meissner, Amelia, 107
Midway Plaisance (World's Columbian Exposition), 74, 75
Missouri school exhibit, at the Philadelphia Centennial Exposition, content of 31-33
Morgan, Thomas J., 76, 78
Moscow Imperial Technical School, exhibit at the Philadelphia Centennial Exposition, 23-28

Nast, Thomas, 18
National Museum (Smithsonian), 51
Native American Education exhibit, at the Louisiana Purchase Exposition, 116-118
Native American school exhibit, at the World's Columbian Exposition, 76
New York College for the Training of Teachers, 90
Northern Home for friendless children (Philadelphia), 36
Northrup, B. G., 17, 43-45

Ontario Educational exhibit, at the Philadelphia Centennial Exposition, 33, 48
Orientalism, 133

Palace of Education (Louisiana Purchase Exposition), 102, 103. 120
Palmer, Potter, 68
Pan American Exposition (1901), 7
Peabody, Elizabeth Palmer, 35, 36, 38

Peabody Museum of American Archaeology and Ethnology (Cambridge, MA), 74
Pedagogic Museum (St. Petersburg), 47, 48
Pennsylvania Educational exhibit, at the Philadelphia Centennial Exposition, 39-40
Philadelphia Centennial Exposition (1876), education exhibits, 16-55; Chinese exhibit, 46; contemporary accounts of the educational exhibits, 19; French educational exhibit, 16; International Conference on Education, 40-41;Japanese educational exhibit, 46-47;Kindergarten exhibits, 33-39; Machinery Hall, 23; Massachusetts Art exhibit, 31; Missouri school exhibit, content of, 31-33; Moscow Imperial Technical School, exhibit, 23-28; Ontario Educational exhibit, 33, 48; Pennsylvania Educational exhibit, 39-40; Russian Industrial Education exhibits, 23; Swedish schoolhouse, 19-21;
Philbert, Edmund, 104
Philbrick, John, 20
Philippine exhibit, at the Louisiana Purchase Exposition, 112-116; demonstration classes, 115
Phonograph, use of in education, 83-84
"Pike" (Louisiana Purchase Exposition, St. Louis), 74
Pledge of Allegiance, 68, 69
Pratt, Richard Henry, 77
Progress, education as key to, 52, 55, 100
Putnam, Frederick Ward, 74, 76, 77, 78

Racism, at the Louisiana Purchase Exposition, 114
Rathmann, Carl, 106
Rogers, Howard, 102, 103, 121
Roosevelt, Theodore, 101, 112
Root, Elihu, 112
Ross, G. W., 81
Royce, Josiah, 82, 100
Rydell, Robert W., 5, 67, 69, 73, 75, 113
Runkle, John D., 25–28
Russian Industrial Education exhibits, at the Philadelphia Centennial Exposition, 23

Said, Edward, 133–134
Saint Louis Public Schools exhibit (Louisiana Purchase Exposition), 104–106
Saint Louis Public Schools Educational Museum, 106–107, 108
Salmon, Otto, 87
Schniederhahn, Edward, 120
Self-made man, tradition of, 17
Senborn, Schwarz, Baron, 9
Sheppard, J. J., 124
Sickles, Emma, 78
Skiff, Frederick J., 100, 131
Sloyd (manual training system), at the World's Columbian Exposition, 83, 86–90
Sloyd Training School (Boston), 88
Smith, Frank Webster, 99
Smith, Walter, 28
Smithsonian Institution, 51, 65
Smithsonian Institution (at the Louisiana Purchase Exposition, Saint Louis), 109, Anthropological exhibit, 110–112; Astrophysical Observatory, 110; Children's Room, 109; National Zoological Park, 110
Smithsonian Institution (at the World's Columbian Exposition, Chicago), 74
Snider, Denton J., 73
Soldan, F. Louis, 106
Sounders, William, 51
South Kensington Museum, 7
Statistics, educational, 41
Stevens Institute of Technology, 22
Swedish exhibit, at the World's Columbian Exposition, 83
Swedish schoolhouse, at the Philadelphia Centennial Exposition, 19–21

Taft, William Howard, 112
Turner, Frederick Jackson, 65

United States, transformation from an agrarian to an urban and industrialized society, 3

Victoria, Queen, 7
Viennese Exposition (1873), 9; educational exhibits, 9, 10
Violle, Jules, 79

Waetzoldt, Stephen, 79, 83, 84
Waterman Jr., Richard, 91
White, E. E., 55
"White City", 66
Wickersham, J. P., 33
Wilson, William P., 113
Wilson, Woodrow, 82, 100
Winthrop, John, 72
Woodward, Calvin M., 27, 90, 118
Woman's Building, at the World's Columbian Exposition, 93
Worcester County Free Institute of Industrial Science, 22
World's Columbian Exposition (Chicago, 1893), 64–96; as a symbolic construct, 73; as an illustrated ency-

clopedia of civilization, 67; Bureau of Indian Affairs' exhibit, 78;Carlisle School, 77; Catholic Educational exhibit, 84–86; Children's Building, 83; classification of exhibits, 65, 67; cliff dwellers exhibit, 76; Educational Congress, 80;ethnological displays, 74–76; German Educational exhibit, 82–83; Liberal Arts building, 70; "Living" exhibits, 75; Mechanical Arts Palace, 66; Midway Plaisance, 74, 75; Native American school exhibit, 76; Sloyd (manual training system), 83, 86–90;Smithsonian Institution, 74;Swedish exhibit, 83;woman's Building, 83; World Congresses, 80

World Congresses, at the World's Columbian Exposition, 80

Wright, Frank Lloyd, 37

THIS SERIES EXPLORES THE HISTORY OF SCHOOLS AND SCHOOLING in the United States and other countries. Books in this series examine the historical development of schools and educational processes, with special emphasis on issues of educational policy, curriculum and pedagogy, as well as issues relating to race, class, gender, and ethnicity. Special emphasis will be placed on the lessons to be learned from the past for contemporary educational reform and policy. Although the series will publish books related to education in the broadest societal and cultural context, it especially seeks books on the history of specific schools and on the lives of educational leaders and school founders.

For additional information about this series or for the submission of manuscripts, please contact the general editors:

Alan R. Sadovnik
Rutgers University-Newark
Education Dept.
155 Conklin Hall
175 University Avenue
Newark, NJ 07102

Susan F. Semel
The City College of New York, CUNY
138th Street and Convent Avenue
NAC 5/208
New York, NY 10031

To order other books in this series, please contact our Customer Service Department:

800-770-LANG (within the U.S.)
212-647-7706 (outside the U.S.)
212-647-7707 FAX

Or browse online by series at:

www.peterlang.com

www.ingramcontent.com/pod-product-compliance
Ingram Content Group UK Ltd.
Pitfield, Milton Keynes, MK11 3LW, UK
UKHW022239230426
12048UKWH00018BA/1360